SEEDS OF GREATNESS
15 Seeds to Plant for Harvesting Your Greatness

Written by CJ Gross

Foreword by Willie Jolley

PENDIUM

PUBLISHING HOUSE
514-201 Daniels Street
Raleigh, NC 27605

For information, please visit our Web site at
www.pendiumpublishing.com

PENDIUM Publishing and its logo
are registered trademarks.

Seeds of Greatness
By CJ Gross

Copyright © CJ Gross, 2011
All Rights Reserved.

ISBN: 978-1-936513-16-1

Table of Contents

Thank You

To my mother, Ella J. Gross who taught me to never give up, be patient, work things out and trust in GOD. Thank you for all of the unconditional love.

To my father, John F. Gross, who taught me to be present, to show up no matter what: rain, sleet, snow or earthquake. Thank you for being there for my children, my dreams, my goals and myself.

To my sister and friend, Selina L. Gross, who taught me to plan, to meditate, and to seek inner truth.

To my daughters Phallen, Christen and Lauren for teaching me how to become a better parent; for assisting me at workshops, community fairs, and book signings; and for listening to all those self-help audio programs in the car.

To Willie Jolley, who inspired me to start on my journey in personal development.

To A-Nisaa Harper, for her inspiration to work on my book day and night until it was done.

To my editorial team, Kay Shopskire, Janice Cummings, Jeanita Morrris and Brandy Whyte.

To GOD, for giving me the innate talent, skills and abilities necessary for my journey in life and the vision for this book.

To the First Friday's Mastermind Group, who has supported me through the publishing phase of this book.

And to everyone else who have supported me along my journey.

Sponsors

Without each and every individual and company sponsor below, this book would not be possible.

Thank you sponsors!!!

Selina Gross
Bowie, MD

Brandy Whyte
Owings Mills, MD

Wilson & Stephanie Cox
Clinton, MD

Gregory and Wakina Scott
Accokeek, MD

Cassandra Nwosu, Author of "Living the I Am"
Baltimore, MD

Tracy Oliver-Keyser, Embracing the Journey, LLC
Baltimore, MD

Reginald Ready
Upper Marlboro, MD

Juneous A. Pettijohn, Transforming U, LLC
Upper Marlboro, MD

Nia F. Johnson
Suitland, MD

Sarah Tilmen
Alpharetta, GA

The Keys to Canaan

Enlightening Parents to Nurture Healthy Families

The Keys to Canaan was founded in 2004. Our mission is to enlighten parents to nurture healthy families. Our vision is for parents to love themselves and their families, so they can develop strong and resilient families, and build thriving, self-sufficient and empowered communities. Our programs include:

- One-on-One Life Coaching for Parents
- Adult Basic Education
- Benning Terrace Family Exercise and Nutrition
- Barry Farm Family Exercise and Nutrition
- DC Fatherhood Initiative Program/Job Readiness Support Group

Please feel free to contact us for details about our work in the community.

834 Hilltop Terrace, SE, Washington, DC 20019
202-583-0992 • info3@cfaith.com •
www.thekeystocanaan.org

Foreword
By Willie Jolley

I met CJ Gross at the Washington D.C., National Speakers Association meeting and I was impressed with his tenacity when he made sure to get his question answered in the midst of a very competitive question and answer segment. I was equally impressed with CJ's level of persistence in trying to find a way to partner with me on a project, which he accomplished when we did a local radio show on parenting. I believe CJ Gross possesses the passion, desire, and commitment that it takes to assist others in developing the determination that it takes to live their dreams. This book shares those secrets in a magnificent way.

I have read many books but this book is unique. CJ Gross shares his success secrets and it's like having your very own coach with you all the time. This book is a great read for the person who wants to live their life to the fullest and use their God-given talents to the fullest. It is for the person who is ready to make meaningful and powerful decisions in their life. It is for the person that wants to make a grand difference in the world!

Success is attracted to those who have clarity about what they want and possess a strong reason as to why they want it. I believe that if you have strong enough "whys" you can find the "hows!" Reading this book will not only inspire you to achieve success but it will also assist you in putting together a sure fire plan for cultivating the greatness that dwells within you. The exercises in this book will lend to self-discovery that will broaden your perspective about what is possible for your personal and professional goals and dreams.

This book provides an arsenal of support for those who are ready to be awakened to their greatness!!! From your success, others will see that it is not only possibly but do-able and will be inspired to read the book and get their lives going in the right direction. I recommend you read this book, then re-read it to make sure you got all the pearls that CJ has shared, then tell your friends about the book. Gandhi said, "Be the change you want to see in the world!" Therefore the first step to greatness starts with self and then you can help someone else! Start today by reading this book and moving on to changing your future and your families. I highly recommend this book!

Willie Jolley, Best Selling Author of "A Setback Is A Setup For A Comeback" and "Turn Setbacks Into Greenbacks," and Award Winning Speaker and Media Personality!

Introduction

Hello Great Ones!!!

Have you ever said to yourself, "there has to be more to life than this?" Most people have asked themselves this question but unfortunately they have not found the "more to life" that they seek. Often times they do not think it is possible to have a better life than what they are exposed to daily. Despite previous thoughts of self-doubt or failure, I am here to tell you that you can have the life you desire. In fact you are living that life right now. Yes, the very life you say you want is manifesting itself right before your very eyes. You might be saying to yourself, "This guy is crazy," but keep reading and I will prove that you are getting everything you want and if not, it is shortly on its way to you. When I conduct workshops all across the country I ask my audiences the same question and I always get the "this guy must be crazy" look. You know what? The audiences are correct! I am *crazy*, but I am also right and the audiences are pleasantly surprised once I prove it to them. For example, let's say you are looking for a new job so you tell your friends and family members that you are doing so. You then search the Internet to submit your resume to prospective jobs. You are now waiting for the overwhelming number of telephone calls from potential employers to schedule interviews...but those phone calls never come. Why is this so? Because you have only "said" you want a new job but you have not done what it takes to manifest it into reality. If you are not getting what you want, then you are not doing what it takes to make it happen.

Everything you have really wanted and have obtained in life, you have worked hard to manifest it into reality. Whether it was making numerous phone calls to close a sell; sending hundreds of resumes out to land the perfect job; staying up all night to finish a report to win a bid or pass a class; carving quality time out of your busy schedule for your family; spending more time in meditation to hear God; or just being steadfast enough to complete your first book you did what it took to make it happen. As for the things you did not get but *said* you wanted, the honest truth is, you really did not want them. If you did, you would have done whatever it took to make it happen; **you would have taken more action**.

Action is the tool every person must use to bring their goals and dreams into reality. In order to attain the things you really want you must take action to get results; sometimes the results are instant and for others it may take time to come into fruition. Really big goals and dreams may even take a lifetime. For example, American film director and animator, Walt Disney, died before he saw his dream of the Walt Disney

World Resort manifest into reality. Reverend Martin Luther King, Jr died before he saw the first African American President of the United States and other accomplishments of his work manifest into reality. These men were great men; men of vision; men that had passion for their dream; men that took **action** so their dreams could manifest into reality. As a result, their dreams continue to benefit the entire world.

To be great you must have a dream and take action on it and never give up until it becomes true. For this dream you must be willing to give your time, your energy, your money and for the really big ones, your life. That is what this book is about, harvesting your greatness. **ARE YOU READY TO BECOME GREAT?**

About the Author

My name is Christopher Jabbar Gross but most refer to me as C.J. Gross. I am a Certified Life Coach, Inspirational Speaker,

Mentor, and Author. I speak at private businesses, government agencies, youth centers, schools, churches and community-based organizations on Team Building, Youth/Parental Development and Personal Development. I also conduct one-on-one coaching for individuals to support their personal and professional growth. I have held positions as a Soda Can Recycler, Newspaper Boy, Lawn Care Specialist, Car Care Technician, Personal Assistant, Strawberry Picker, Fast Food Cook, Early Learning Child Care Aid, Package Handler, Grocery Store Stocker, Pizza Deliverer, Drafter, Mechanical Designer, Summer Camp Director, Case Manager, Program Coordinator, Waiter, Dish Washer, High School Teacher, Workshop Leader, Art Consultant/Framer, Door-to-Door Salesman, Demolition Construction Worker, Community Outreach Leader, Community Engagement Coordinator and Mentor Coordinator. I have owned and operated four businesses: a Laundromat in Washington D.C. (Wash Laundromat), a non-profit in Prince George's County, Maryland (U-Life, Inc.), a residential and commercial cleaning company in Forestville, Maryland (Pristine Cleaning Service), and now Seeds of Life, LLC, a national personal and professional development company. In addition, I have appeared on television, radio and have written articles for various newspapers and magazines. In 2009, I published my first book *The Parent Connection: 20 Principles for Strong Parenting.* And finally, I am blessed to have three beautiful daughters and to have sustained a marriage for 11 years.

My road to greatness started March 31, 1974, in Washington, D.C. where I was born. I grew up outside the District in Fort Washington, Maryland. When I was about ten years old I realized I was not like everyone else. I did not act like everyone else; I did not think like everyone else; and more importantly, I did not learn like everyone else, which made school extremely difficult for me. In fact, I hated school. It made me sick just thinking about it. It was not until after taking note of the success of a famous motivational speaker, Willie Jolley, and reading my first book at 25 years old that I was diagnosed with Dyslexia, a learning disability that impacts my ability to read and comprehend words. This was a turning point in my life. I realized that I had been wearing blinders. I saw the world totally different, but most importantly, I saw myself different. The first books I completed were the biographies of Fredrick Douglass, Harriet Tubman and Madam C.J. Walker. I then read *As a Man Thinketh* by James Allen and *Think and Grow Rich* by Napoleon Hill. These books started to cultivate in me a sense of direction and purpose about life. **They awakened my spirit!**

I felt like a slave who had just been granted his freedom and I wanted to share the news with everyone I came in contact with. At this point, I was inspired to retake the entrance exam at a local community college that I previously failed. After taking the test the second time I received an honor score. I then purchased my first home with no money down and with the money received at the closing table, I purchased *Wash*

Laundromat with the help of family. At this point I started to wonder if anyone else knew about this powerful life changing information. I wished I had my hands on this information when I was a child; I wouldn't have struggled so much in school. I was then inspired to begin U-Life, Incorporated, a non-profit organization that provided mentoring and life skills workshops for youth in Prince George's County, Maryland. Through my work with the youth I realized that in order to influence change in the youth, their parents must be armed with support, skills, and knowledge. As a result, parental coaching became another service that was offered through U-Life, Incorporated. I was then inspired to broaden my life coaching services to meet the personal/professional development needs of all people through Seeds of Life, LLC, a national personal development company. I am currently a full-time life coach, speaker, and author. I have embarked on a wonderful journey of assisting others to breathe life into their own dreams and seeing the greatness within themselves. This book is my offering to you. It is filled with fifteen seeds that, if planted and nurtured, will harvest your greatness and reap a harvest that you and the world will benefit from.

I am a living testimony to the fact that it does not matter about your childhood, education level, skin color, social-economic status, religion, gender, sexual orientation, height, geographic location, or disability if you want to be great, you can!

Welcome to the journey!

SEEDS OF GREATNESS
15 Seeds to Plant for Harvesting Your Greatness

The Seed of a Dream

"It does not take courage to dream, but it does take courage to make your dreams come true."

What Happened to Your Dreams?

Remember when you dreamt about what you were going to do when you grew up? How about the kind of house you would own or how much money you would make and your parents said you could have and do anything you wanted? Then you grew up and realized that dreams only come true in fairytales.

Eventually most adults are faced with the challenges of living in the real world and dealing with real problems. Unfortunately, most adults don't have real solutions or at least solutions that will effectively resolve their problems and still allow them to pursue their dreams. So to answer the question, "What happened to your dreams?" Life happened and you did not have enough support, ingenuity, skills, or faith, in your dreams-- so you gave up.

The Dream of a Great Job:

Do you work in a less than desirable job or career? Do you find yourself daydreaming during the company meeting as your supervisor discusses the companies policy and procedure manual. You opt to stay at an unfulfilling job out of necessity and to pay bills, but ultimately you are only making yourself and those around you miserable.

The Dream of a Relationship:

Do you wake up next to a person who was the *best thing since sliced bread* when you met them, but now they remind you of molded bread with smelly cheese on top? The thought of leaving enters your mind but you are reminded that in the case of a separation or divorce your partner will get half of your assets and you will no longer have anyone to listen to your problems. So you remain unhappy to avoid confronting your fears and worries. Every once in a while you think, "Whatever happened to the happily ever after story?" All while feeling deceived and hoodwinked.

The Dream of an Education:

Do you go to school and think, "Am I in the wrong place? How come the teacher doesn't see my talents?" While reflecting, you realize that you don't like your major, yet you stay on the path so that you don't disappoint your teachers or parents.

The Dream of an Opportunity:

Do you wake up in a concrete cell that is one of hundreds housing others that have made misguided decisions? You know if given the right circumstances, you could not only change your life, you could change the world, but you feel you lack the proper resources to make your dreams come true.

The Dream of Purpose in Life:
Are you just sick of your dreary and mundane existence? Do you want to start living your dreams and give your life some meaning?

The Dream Realized:
You are living your dreams and just want to live more of it.

Whatever your circumstance, it's imperative that you recognize one concept: **your most powerful asset is your dreams**. Your dreams are more precious than diamonds, more valuable than money, more fulfilling than the finest cuisine, and if you believe in them they will light the way to freedom, happiness, and success. The ability to dream is your ticket to a front row seat of what your future can look like if you can exercise just a little faith.

Anything that has manifested into reality starts as a dream. A dream is a psychological blueprint of possibility that can harness the emotional force of creativity, which can help its owner overcome any obstacle standing in the way of manifestation. To be great, you must possess the ability to see the intangible in your mind then muster the courage it takes to embark on the journey of faith into the unknown.

3

Find the Right Dream to Follow

The dream that will make you great is the dream that reappears in every part of your life. Whether you are asleep, at work, at school, at play and even in the midst of difficult situations, these dreams appear and are always speaking to you. I call these dreams **Mega Dreams**, or as Anthony Robbins said in his book, <u>Awaken the Giant Within</u>, your *magnificent obsession*. These dreams can take you to new heights if you follow them.

The Sacrifice

To follow your Mega Dream is to sacrifice your life. A person cannot become great unless he or she is willing to allow their Mega Dream to guide their life. In this process a person can find their true purpose and life takes on a new meaning. After this discovery it is not uncommon to hear a person say their life is filled with purpose. Every aspect of life revolves around the Mega Dream for those who choose to accept the gift. Life becomes clear, fear of taking action dissipates, and providence reveals itself. The only real sacrifice you have to make is letting go of the fear that impedes your life.

Never Let Go of the Dream

Never let go of the dream of the future you would like to have for you and/or your family. Your dream keeps you alive. A dream has the ability to keep you focused and moving forward in life. For some people a dream is just that, a dream. It's only something they do when they are sleep. The true dreamers dream with their eyes wide open. They see and speak of their dreams as if they are already reality. Dreams give their owners motivation, inspiration and it is the reason why they put themselves through all of the agony and pain it takes to manifest them.

Your dream is like a kite. You have picked it because it is beautiful to you and you believe in it like no one else. You believe that it can soar and fly high into the sky above the clouds. It is your job to get your kite off the ground and into the air. Unfortunately, some days there will not be enough wind to carry your kite up into the sky. On the days when there is not enough wind, and there will be plenty of those, you must run! I did not say walk or jog, I said run. Run like it is all that you have in life to do. Run like you have never run before. Run as if you are being chase by a hungry lion. Run as if your life depended on it. More importantly, run so you can fly your kite high in the sky for all to see. When you fly your kite high in the sky regardless whether there's enough wind to take it up or not, you give others the courage, motivation, and inspiration to do the same thing. Don't die with your dreams bottled up inside of you. Your dreams whatever they are will make the world a better place to live in.

The consequence of not chasing your dreams is becoming one of the many walking dead. The walking dead are the people that have slipped into mediocrity. They have allowed the worries and dramas of life to subdue their passion about their dream. When you let your dream go the hope of something great happening dies. The result is stagnation and mediocrity. When you are not passionate about life you began to have low energy, you become sick more often, and you may develop a negative attitude towards life and relationships and you will become an unconscious dream buster for others.

Life is in the dream, never let go of it!

The Birth of a Dream

A dream needs to be birthed just like a baby. Just like a baby a dream needs time to fully develop before it can be brought into the real world. Just like a baby a dream needs constant nurturing before it can become self-sufficient. In order to survive dreams need nurturing and a vision for how it will survive in the real world or it will die. That's why most dreams are aborted before birth; there is no vision for the future of it in the mind of its parent. Sometimes there is great pain evolved with birthing a dream, but it is nothing compared to the pain the parent will face years later if it is not brought into reality. There is a reason why you were giving your dream; the only way to truly find out why, is to birth it.

Quotes from Dreamers

"Your heart will lead you to your dreams and your head will lead you to your fears."

Unknown

"Search your heart for the dreams you've overlooked"
Unknown

"A goal is a dream with a deadline."
Napoleon Hill

"Happy are those who dream dreams and are ready to pay the price to make them come true."
Leon Joseph Cardinal Suenens

"Every great dream begins with a dreamer. Always remember, you have within you the strength, the patience, and the passion to reach for the stars to change the world."
Harriet Tubman

<u>Great Dreamers to Research</u>

Frederick Douglass – Abolitionist, Orator, Real Estate Investor and Writer
Frank Lloyd Wright - Architect
Albert Einstein - Physicist
Walt Disney – Creator of Mickey Mouse and founder of Disneyland and Walt Disney World
Barack Obama- 44th President of the United States
Leonardo Da Vinci - Inventor, Painter, Sculptor, Architect, Engineer, and Scientist
Thomas Edison – Inventor and Entrepreneur
Sean 'P. Diddy' Combs – Urban Entertainer and Entrepreneur

The Seed of a Dream

Henry Ford - Ford Motor Company Founder

Madam C.J. Walker – Women's Hair Care Consultant and Entrepreneur

Ray Kroc – Businessman and McDonald's Founder

Martin Luther King Jr. – Pastor and Civil Rights Leader

<u>Here are Some Questions to Assist with Identifying Your Dream</u>:

1. What would you do with your life if money did not matter?

_____

_____

2. Once you have identified what you would do with your life if money were not an issue, ask yourself the inquisitive *whys*. Repeatedly ask yourself *why* you want to make this change for your life and each time you answer challenge yourself to respond differently. If you cannot think of eight or ten different reasons you may want to do more research and take time to ponder over what you really want for your life. If you need help, sit down with a person you respect for some guidance.

_____

_____

3. What are your reoccurring dreams?

_____

_____

4. What do you feel is holding you back from pursuing your dreams?

_____

_____

5. Imagine you only had six months to live. Where would you go? Who would you meet? What kind of legacy would you want to leave behind? What would you want people to say about you at your funeral?

_____

_____

6. What special gifts and talents do you possess that can potentially improve society?

_____

_____

7. Tip: Keep a pen and paper or voice recorder by your bed, in your office, and on your person so that you can keep track of your reoccurring dreams.

_____

_____

The Seed of Action

1. Create a dream board. A dream board is a collage made on cardboard, construction paper, or any other medium of any size. Your task is to find photos, images, words that represent your dream. Then take those images and glue, staple, or tape it to the board. The photos should be as vivid and specific as possible. You can use photos that you have taken or you can cut them out of a magazine. You can also use words to support the photos. **This activity is very important.** It will keep you conscious of your dreams and what you want out of life. It really works! Just try it; what do you have to lose?

The Seed of a Goal

"Goals are the stepping stones to your dream"

What is a Goal?

A goal is a written or verbal statement claiming what you want in your possession or a state you wish to achieve. Each goal plays a specific role in helping you get to your overall destination of greatness. Goals are like steps; after you reach one you can go onto the next goal that is positioned at a higher level. Each goal elevates you so you can reach the next one. Achieving your goals also increases your self-confidence and makes you feel more secure about your abilities and skills. Remember, the person you become during the process of reaching your goals is more important than the goals themselves. All of the steps you take to reach your goals will strengthen and build your character. The process of chasing your goals prepares you for the next phase of your journey. The challenges you face hold the key to attaining future goals.

Why Should You Set Goals?

Our goals make it possible to turn dreams into reality. A person without a goal is like a ship at sea with no destination. If you have not written clear and specific goals, you are sure to fail or, at best, live an aimless life. Goals keep you on task and make you accountable for what you say you want. People that do not set goals have an unconscious goal to fail. Look at it this way: People usually set goals that they think they can achieve so if you are not setting any goals at all what does that tell you? The beautiful thing about setting goals is they don't cost anything, they are easy to set, and they don't put you down if you don't reach them. Some of the most successful people in the world, such as Oprah Winfrey, Bill Gates, Donald Trump, Michael Jordan and President Barack Obama set goals. Why shouldn't you?

How to Set Goals?

Begin by setting goals you feel comfortable and confident you can achieve. This will help build your confidence. As you achieve the smaller goals, larger and more complex goals can be set. Make sure your goals are clear, exact and include the following information: color, size, style, time and date of completion, location, who needs to be involved, and why you want to accomplish it. Your goals should be specific and measurable (i.e., I will save 10 percent of my monthly salary for 12 months for a down payment on a home loan). You should write your goals down, keep them in more then one location, and carry them with you every place you go.

Sample Goals

I **_will_** lose 20 lbs. by 4pm, March 31, 2010 so that I can become healthier.

I *will* travel to Hawaii on a Carnival Cruse line with a friend or family member by 4pm April 19, 2011 so that I can experience other cultures and write my next book sitting on the beach sipping Pina Coladas until the sun goes down.

I *will* buy a 2011 red convertible Corvette December 31, 2010, 11:59pm so that I can live out my childhood fantasy.

I *will* move to San Diego, California, and buy a five bedroom, 5,000 square foot house overlooking the ocean for $400,000.00 by March 31, 2011, at 12pm so my wife and I can enjoy our retirement.

I *will* complete my bachelor's degree in Sociology at the University of Maryland by May 2014, so that I can continue my educational development and receive a promotion.

The more specific you are when setting goals, the better the outcome. And remember to include the word "*will*" in your goal statement. When your brain hears "*will*" it thinks in the present tense and works to make your goals real.

The following lists and defines the various types of goals you will utilize to achieve greatness.

Long Term Goals
A long-term goal is one that may take years to accomplish,

such as completing a degree, buying a house, or finding your dream job.

Short Term Goals

A short-term goal is a goal that may take one to twelve months to accomplish such as completing a certification course, losing 20 pounds, or buying a car.

Daily Goals

Daily goals support your bigger goals and ultimately your dreams. Daily goals are things you can get done in one day or on your lunch hour or after work such as phone calls, meetings, e-mails, research and purchases.

Mega Goals

Mega goals are sometimes bigger than life itself. You can spend a lifetime trying to accomplish **Mega Goals** and still fall short of victory. Some people refer to them as dreams because they are so big you can only see them abstractly. In most scenarios you will have to enlist others to help you achieve these goals.

Breakthrough Goals

A breakthrough goal is a goal that, if accomplished, will position you to receive more opportunities in life and free up resources such as time, money and energy. These goals will also motivate you to accomplish larger and more cumbersome goals. Some of these may include increasing your income, losing 40 pounds, getting out of an emotionally draining relationship, cleaning and organizing a room in your house or your office, buying a computer so you can access the internet from home, getting your bachelor's degree, going back to school to earn your GED or High School Diploma, changing your wardrobe or moving to a city that will support your dreams. ***Breakthrough goals are the most powerful goals.*** Breakthrough goals can be difficult to accomplish but are ultimately the most rewarding. They are usually the goals that stretch you the most physically, mentally, and spiritually. To achieve your breakthrough goal you may need to seek out a coach or a mentor. To learn more about mentors and coaches see, <u>The Seed of a Network</u> chapter.

Goal Acceleration

Goal acceleration is the process in which a goal is accomplished in a decreased amount of time. To start accelerating your goals the best methods are to:

- Take a class on your goal

- Read a book on your goal

- Watch a video on your goal

- Listen to a CD program on your goal

- Get a coach or mentor that has achieved the same goal to help you. To learn more about mentors and coaches see, <u>The Seed of a Network</u> chapter.

15

Doing all the above will accelerate your goal.

<u>Here are Some Questions to Ask Yourself to</u>

<u>Begin Setting Goals</u>:

1. Do you currently set goals? If not, why?

_____

_____

2. How often do you set goals?

_____

_____

3. How often do you achieve your goals?

_____

_____

4. In the next 30 to 90 days what goals would you like to achieve?

_____

_____

5. What are some of your breakthrough goals?

    _____

    _____

6. How would you feel if you accomplished all of your breakthrough goals?

    _____

    _____

7. What price are you willing to pay to accomplish your breakthrough goals?

    _____

    _____

The Seeds of Action

1. Write down 10 things you want to have or achieve.

2. Write down the resources you need to accomplish them.

3. Number each goal from 1 to 10 based on the level of importance and value with one being the most valuable and 10 being the least valuable.

4. Do your research on each goal to find out as much as you possibly can (i.e., cost, size, color, style, popularity, location, how to obtain it) and be sure to talk to others that have accomplished this goal.

5. Post your goals on your refrigerator, in your office, over your dresser, on your bathroom mirror and anywhere else you frequently visit.

6. Find an accountability partner you can share your goals with. This partner should be supportive, trust worthy, and goal oriented in his/her own personal and professional life.

7. As previously mentioned, create a dream board. A dream board is a collage or board of any size that has photos of what you want glued, stapled or taped on it. The photos should be as vivid and specific as possible. You can use photos that you have taken or you can cut them out of a magazine. You can also use words to support the photos. **This activity is very important.** It will keep you conscious of what you want out of life and it really works. Just try it what do you have to lose.

8. Stay Motivated. Make sure you are doing something every day to move closer to achieving your goals. Associate yourself with people that are setting and

achieving their goals. Listen to inspirational music and inspirational speakers to give you motivation.

9. Join or create a *Mastermind Group*. A mastermind group is a group of people that meet regularly to discuss their goals. The purpose of this group is to brainstorm and come up with different solutions to support each member in achieving their goals. The benefits of using a mastermind group are endless, not only does it assist you in accomplishing your goals, it allows you to gather information from outside sources that can bring a fresh alternative perspective to your mission that you may not have considered otherwise. To learn more about mastermind groups see the <u>Seeds of a Network</u> chapter.

The Seed of a Plan

" If you don't have a plan, you don't' have a chance!"

Planning Lays the Foundation for Greatness

Without a plan your greatness will only remain potential, unrealized potential. Most people only talk about becoming great; few actually plan to do it. To plan for anything means you are calculating the resources needed, going over the steps in your head that you will have to execute, freeing up time in your schedule, making sure you have the mental energy and stamina necessary, and most of all writing it down. Developing a plan means you are serious about achieving your goals.

In business you cannot get a loan from a bank if you don't have a business plan. Why? Because, a plan tells others and reminds you of what you are going to do, what actions you need to take, who needs to be involved, how much it's going to cost and if it's feasible to move forward now? Plans not only make sense, they make dollars too. Just ask any successful business man or woman. Whether it's business, marriage, losing weight, returning to school, securing a new job, running a marathon, having a baby or getting ready for retirement planning breeds success and great planning breeds great success.

What Happens When You Don't Plan?

When you don't plan you waste valuable time and other resources. Sometimes, it will cost you the project and even worse, respect from others. When you don't plan you are unconsciously saying to yourself and others you are not serious about getting what you say you want. The absence of a plan creates confusion, frustration, and a lack of guidance.

Look at any major successful campaign in history: a military assault, sports championship, a business acquisition, a new product merging on to the scene, a run for the presidency, sailing around the world, obtaining the perfect job or the purchase of a dream home, it all starts with a brilliant plan.

If you don't plan properly you could lose the game; if you don't plan at all you may never get in the game.

What Happens When You Have a Plan and it Doesn't Work?

A plan is simply a proposal of what you want to do or of what you are attempting to do. It is a calculated guess of what you want to do in the future, based on past and present conditions as well as an inventory of your resources, skills sets, and abilities. Plans don't always work out; sometimes they fail miserably. Remember, a plan is a guide or a roadmap for where you want to go in the future.

When your plans don't work the way you want them to it is important not to give up or become frustrated. Plans should always be flexible and have two to three alternative options. For example, if you are planning to go to college on a scholarship, but for whatever reason you don't receive it; you don't give up on going to college, you alter your plan. You find a work study program, put on a fundraiser, apply for other scholarships, get a loan or work a job. Here is another example, you are starting your own business and spent all of your savings investing in a product that doesn't sell. You don't give up; you find a way to recoup your money, you find a new market for the product, you redevelop the product, or you come up with a new product that someone else is willing to fund. Whatever you do, don't give up. Giving up on your plans will set into motion a chain of events, emotions, and conditions that will reinforce negative thoughts of failure; you may believe that you can't have what you want out of life. This can sometimes reaffirm thoughts of inadequacy and self-doubt from childhood or past failures. Failure, flexibility, alternative planning, and overcoming self-doubt are by-products of success.

When your plan doesn't work, you have to re-work, re-calculate, re-think, revive, seek spiritual guidance and move forward because the future holds your blessings.

Making Sure Your Plans Work

Before a new car, video game, television, skin cream or product of any type is placed on the market it is tested, re-tested, and then tested again before it is released to the general public. Why? Because when something is tested you get a private opportunity to see its strengths as well as its weaknesses. Once you know the weakness of a plan, you have opportunity to reevaluate it and redevelop it.

Plans that work best are the ones that have been thought about, talked about and tested out. Here is a question for you: When would you like to find out if your boat can float on the shore or in the middle of the ocean?

Just Imagine

Imagine boarding an airplane, but not just any airplane, a 747 jumbo jet that seats up to 496 passengers. The plane takes off and a few hours after you are in the air you hear the pilot over the loud speakers say, "Unfortunately we did not refuel the plane because we did not estimate how long this trip would take. We have to now turn around and see if we could make it back to our home airport." Could you imagine the confusion, frustration, headaches and inconvenience it would cause to not only you but to everyone on the plane? Think about how many people's plans would have to change and how it would affect their family members, friends, co-workers and finances not to mention their stress levels. Now, due to the inadequate planning by the airline, passengers may not be able to reach their destinations. Furthermore, there is a safety issue and hundreds of lives are at risk.

This is an extreme situation but not difficult to imagine. Here's a question: Do you think the airplane scenario could have been avoided? With proper planning, of course it could. Most plans will not involve 496 people and endanger the lives of others, but neglecting to plan can affect others who are close to you (i.e., family members, friends, co-workers). When you neglect to properly plan you could lose time, money, respect trust, and in this case lives.

Be Consistent

If there is one thing I know for sure, it's that no one can accomplish a major goal or achieve greatness without consistency. Consistency is the continuous motivation that keeps you going in the face of failure and after minute victories have passed. Consistency is your ability to be a constant when everything around you is changing and unstable. It is an agreement to the process of manifestation and it is how great people break down their barriers to success.

In order to be consistent you must have a strong reason to persist against the waves of change and the undercurrent of procrastination. Consistent people know why they are doing what they are doing and have a strong passion for follow-up. If you want to be consistent, you must have strong faith in the incubation process. The incubation process is the period of time you take to dream, make goals, and plan; it is the time you take to meditate with little to no interruptions from outside influences. Without the incubation process the roots of a seed would never break through the earth's soil to start the growth of a Great Oak.

Think about this: if your heart were not consistent you would be dead right now! In other words life itself can't exist without consistency; so how do you think your dreams can exist without consistency?

Be Patient

In order for your plan to work you must exercise patience. That's right, you must endure some mild, or in some cases, severe pain. However, patience is not only about enduring, it is *how* you endure. A true sign of patience is the ability to handle discomfort and still exhibit a great deal of self-control, calmness, and focus on the task at hand. In other words, to be patient is to be mentally, physically, and spiritually accepting of the conditions you must navigate in order to work the plan or accomplish your goal. You must be resilient during times of uncertainty.

Without patience you are sure to fail the most remedial task.

Here are Some Questions to Ask Yourself to Increase Your Planning Skills:

1. How often do you plan? If not often, why not?

_____

_____

2. Are you consistent at working your plan? If not, why not?

_____

_____

3. Are you patient when it comes to seeing your plans through? If not, why not?

_____

_____

4. In the past have your plans been more successful or less successful? Why?

_____

_____

5. How much time do you spend on the planning phase of your goals/projects?

_____

_____

6. Do you think you could or should spend more time in the planning phase of your projects?

_____

_____

7. What are some different things that could help you become a more effective planner (i.e., calendar, planner, a smart phone, a planning workshop, a book on planning)?

_____

_____

8. Identify people who can assist you with developing a successful plan?

_____

_____

9. When your project is less then successful how much time do you spend reflecting on how you could improve it next time?

_____

_____

10. How much more effective could you be if you started planning more?

_____

_____

The Seeds of Action

1. Write down three of your biggest successes and three of your biggest failures. Then identify and write what made it successful or a failure.

2. Join a master mind group to help you with your planning (see previous chapter).

3. Attend two to three different classes/workshops where you can learn different tips, tools and techniques for better planning.

4. Read some books on planning/project management.

5. Listen to an audio program about planning/project management.

6. Take notes while you are working your plan so that you can reflect on them later.

9. Consult with a friend, a mentor or a coach for assistance with planning. For more information on mentors and coaches see the <u>Seeds of a Network</u>.

The Seed of Love

"Love is power, Love is beauty, Love is balance, Love is faith and Love is life."

Love is the most written about, sung about and sought after word in the human language.

The Definitions of Love

Webster's dictionary definition of love:

1. Strong affection
2. Warm attachment
3. Attraction based on sexual desire
4. A beloved person's unselfish loyalty
5. A benevolent concern for others

For the purpose of this book, I will be using the following definition for love: *A strong undeniable and sometimes overwhelming feeling/emotion of willingness to sacrifice money, time, energy, status, material things and sometimes life itself to allure, acquire, and or conquer a person, place or thing.*

What's Love Got to do with it?

Love has everything to do with all things. Greatness itself is derived from love. An athlete becomes great because of their love for sports; doctors become great because of their love for helping people with their medical needs; artists become great because of their love for creating beautiful artwork; singers, songwriters and musicians become great because of their love for music; entrepreneurs become great because of their love for business; counselors become great because of their love for helping people with social, emotional, and mental issues, and so on. If you want to become great you must find your love.

What do You Love?

What do you love to the point that you are willing to make a sacrifice? What gives you joy in life? What do you think you were put on this earth to do or create? The thing that will make you great is also the thing that will make you the happiest, the most successful, and filled with excitement for life. To find your love you must find your anointment or your GOD given innate gift. This anointment will not only make you happy, it will also support you in finding the right career, the right mate, and the right lifestyle that is just right for you. When you find this gift you will find your greatest love of all--the love of self, the real *you* that came into this world not afraid to take risks, not afraid to express oneself, not afraid to chase dreams, and not afraid to become great. The greatest love that you will ever have is the love you have for what the creator has anointed you with, your GOD given innate gift. Find and embrace this love and every other love in your life will be enriched and fall into place.

Here are Some Questions to Ask Yourself About Your Love:

1. What do you believe you were created for?

   _____

   _____

2. What hobby, sport or other interest do you love but don't do anymore and why?

   _____

   _____

3. What hobby, sport or other interest would you like to fall back in love with?

   _____

   _____

4. What hobby, sport or other interest do you love so much you would do it all day for free?

   _____

   _____

5. How could you turn your love into a consulting business or incorporate it in your current job?

_____

_____

6. If you wrote a book on your love would it be a best seller?

_____

_____

7. If you gave a speech about your love, what would it entail?

_____

_____

8. How can you make sure your love doesn't fade?

_____

_____

The Seeds of Action

1. Take a personality or temperament assessment to help determine your innate talents, abilities and gifts. You can find several on-line personality or temperament

assessment tools that you can use. The one I find most helpful is the Keirsey Temperament Sorter-II which can be found at www.advisorteam.com.

2. Hire a life coach or find a mentor to help you. To learn more about life coaching and mentoring see the Seeds of a Network.

3. Find a School Counselor, Career Counselor, or Spiritual Counselor to help you find your innate talents, abilities, and gifts.

4. Talk to a friend to get their opinion on what they think you would be good at.

5. Meditate and pray. Take 5-10 minutes a day to meditate, be still, clear your mind and listen to what GOD is telling you.

The Seed of Time

"The greatest similarity between a millionaire and a person living in poverty is they both have 24 hours in a day; the greatest difference is what they do with it."

Your Time is the Most Valuable Commodity You Have

Time is the one commodity that you cannot borrow, sell, trade or buy. It is as precious as life. In fact, time is life. Most people take their time for granted. But time is actually like precious coins that you should spend very wisely because you will never get them back and you don't know how many you have to spend. You will live and die for whatever you spend most of your time on in this life, This is true because time sustains life; without time life would not be possible. If you spend most of your time chasing material things, life becomes materialistic; if you spend most of your time worrying about your fears, life becomes fearful; if you spend most of your time serving others with your GOD given gifts, your life becomes great. So, the question becomes what do you spend most of your time on?

The average person throws their time away like pennies on a side walk as if they do not see the value in it. For something as trivial as an argument, the average person will give you a whole hour of their time. If you have an existing relationship with someone they may be more inclined to give you as much as a whole day. When people spend time talking about, thinking about, and writing letters about a situation they are not willing or able to change, it is a disservice to their very existence. People that are destined for greatness know the value of their time and are not willing to spend it wastefully on just anything life shoves their way such as any job, any relationship, or any lifestyle. Once you know the value of your time, you are ready for goal attainment. Time spent on worthwhile activities is the price for greatness.

The matters you chose to spend hours on will turn into days; days will turn into months; months will turn into years and before you know it, you will have spent your entire life on less than worthwhile activities. Hopefully, you will choose to spend this time on achieving greatness rather than pondering over trivial issues, worries, or concerns.

Time Management

I don't understand why this concept is referred to as "time management" because no one actually *manages* time. Time is a continuous flow of the present moving from the past into the future. The present is the cradle between the two. The only thing you can really *manage* is how well you handle the situations in your life. The way you chose to handle situations will determine how you spend your time. Time management is really the ability to maximize your time. You can manage your time by consciously making decisions that increase the quality of your life. To manage your time properly you must be able to answer the following questions:

What do you really value out of life? (i.e., people, spending time a certain environments, spiritual activities)

What tasks, duties, or projects do you need to delegate to others because it's not worth your time?

What task, duties, or projects do you need to complete quickly?

How can you get someone else to do what you don't want to do? (i.e., offer payment, inspire, barter)

The Seven Biggest Time Wasters
1. Watching unproductive television shows (i.e., trashy talk shows, addictive soap operas, reality television).
2. Allowing unimportant telephone conversations interrupt productive activities.
3. The inability to delegate work at home and or in the office.
4. Not making decisions you know you need to make.
5. The inability to say "No" when you do not have the time to commit to the task.
6. Engaging in unproductive conversations with unproductive individuals.
7. Failing to make plans for how you want to live your life.

24 Hour Time Line

On the next page, you will find an example of a <u>24 Hour Time Line</u> which will help you keep track of your time as well as make sure you're spending your time wisely.

Instructions for Using the Timeline:

In each vertical column labeled "Activities", write what you spend time doing on an average day. This will include sleeping, getting ready for work, traveling to work, traveling from work, dinner, helping the children with homework, talking on the phone, attending a class, watching television, reading a book, etc. In the vertical column labeled "Benefits," write the advantage of each activity. For example, the benefit for *sleep* may be *rest* and the benefit of *getting ready for work* may be *preparation.* Other examples include the following:

Activities	Benefits
Work	Supports the family/increases career experience
Watching a soap opera	No benefit
Reading a book	Strengthens my relationships
School	Increases my knowledge / supports employability

In the columns labeled "Level," decide how that activity impacts your quality of life with the following descriptions: 1) *Increases the quality of my life*, 2) *Grows and enhances me*, and 3) *Steals my energy.* For the activities you have to engage in, stretch your mind and search for one or two benefits. Any activity that does not benefit you and/or steals your energy should be replaced with a new or better way of doing this activity. To replace an old activity, think about what activity you would like to replace it with and set it as a goal. For more information about goal setting see the Seeds of a Goal chapter.

24 Hour Time Line Diagram

	Time	Activities	Benefits	Level
AM	12			
	1			
	2			
	3			
	4			
	5			
	6			
	7			
	8			
	9			
	10			
	11			
PM	12			
	1			
	2			
	3			
	4			
	5			
	6			
	7			
	8			
	9			
	10			
	11			

<u>Here are Some Questions to Ask Yourself About How You Spend Your Time</u>:

1. Are you happy with your life?

   _____

   _____

2. If no, what are you doing about it?

   _____

   _____

3. Given 24 hours of a day, how much time do you spend on researching what you want out of life?

   _____

   _____

4. How much time do you spend writing down your goals and what you want to do with your life?

   _____

   _____

5. How much time do you spend developing yourself by attending personal development workshops/trainings, reading books that allow for growth not just

entertainment, and listening to CD programs that inspire you?

_____

_____

6. How many people do you talk to on the phone on any given day that has the resources and or mental wherewithal to support your dreams and goals?

_____

_____

7. How many people have you given your time, money and or services **_freely_** to in order to support their dreams and goals?

_____

_____

8. If you only had six months to live, what would you do different in your life?

_____

_____

The Seeds of Action

Here are some areas to consider spending time on to increase the quality of your life:

1. Take Time for Incubation

    Incubation time is the time you spend on nurturing your thoughts with little to no interruptions. This would also include meditation.

2. Take Time to Love

    Love is the most powerful four letter word in the human language. To love is to be connected with the creator. Love does not have to be hard. In fact, it is one of the easiest things to do. When you were born you had no problems giving and receiving love.

3. Take Time to Cry

    Take time to experience remorse for what you have lost and open your heart for something new to come into your life. Allow the past to be released as you make room for the gifts of the present. Giving yourself permission to weep, feel, and express those emotions is healthy and productive. It allows you to feel the pain and joy of grief. Crying or weeping can release old baggage, settle your physiology, and get you ready to receive something great.

4. Take Time to Write

    Take the time to write your thoughts; feelings; goals, dreams; and even; your mistakes. As you document your thoughts you will invoke new and clearer thoughts. Each time you write, you pour a little bit of yourself out onto the paper giving God an opportunity to pour something great back into you. As you reflect on your thoughts, feelings, goals, dreams, and mistakes you will be able to see your growth right before your eyes.

5. Take Time to Laugh

   Laughing is one of the best ways of reducing stress. Laughing releases feel good endorphins that naturally improve mood. You do not even have to go to the comedy club to find it; all you have to do is find the ironic humor in the smallest of situations.

6. Take Time to Teach and Learn Something New

   Become a lifelong learner by enrolling in classes that teach you something new and interesting. This will broaden your experiences and ability to relate to other people and situations that can catapult you towards your goals and dreams.

7. Take Time to be Industrious.

   Take time to create a bookshelf, a play, an article of clothing, a piece of art, a piece of machinery, a much needed business, or anything that will make your life, community, and society a better place.

8. Take Time to Engage in and Cultivate Healthy Relationships

   People are made to have relationships; that is why

GOD put more than one person on the planet. A healthy relationship can not only drastically increase the quality of your life, but you can also create an opportunity to share your goals and dreams with someone who encourages you. For more information on relationships see the Seed of a Network chapter.

9. Take Time to Exercise

Exercise has multiple benefits. Exercising can reduce stress, high blood pressure, cholesterol, and make you feel great. Exercise can also support creative thinking, as well as increase your life span. GOT EXERCISE?

10. Take Time to Celebrate Life

Make sure you do not let one day pass by without celebrating the gift of life. The celebration could be a dance, making a new friend, laughter, taking a day off from work, being of service to someone else, taking a deep breath or something as simple as a smile.

The Seed of a Network

"You are only as good as your network."

What is a Network?

Your network is a group of people connected to you through various types of relationships, including but not limited to friends, family, coworkers, business associates, teachers, neighbors, clients, dentist, ex-spouses, your child's basketball coach, your child's babysitter, your mechanic, the bus driver, a friend's girlfriend, a co-worker, an old boss, a store clerk, and the list goes on.

A network is an endless number of people that are connected to you, who share a wealth of knowledge and other valuable resources, that if properly leveraged can be accessed by you if you understand the nature and value of your network. Most people consider a friend that knows a lot of people a social butterfly or someone that goes to a lot of parties. Nothing could be further from the truth. A friend, family member, business associate or anyone who knows a large number of people are key people to have or to invite into your network. These individuals can make finding what you need and or want easier, time efficient, and more cost effective than if you were to try all by yourself.

When I worked as a case manager, I could always tell which clients case would demand a higher level of case management support based on the examination of their support network. The stronger the client's network, the need for intense level of case management services decreased. If the client had a strong network, that meant they had access to resources such as money for bus fare, clothing for an interview, a babysitter, a place to stay, or more importantly emotional support. When a person has a strong network they have a safety net. In other words, if the individual fail, they will only fall as far as their network will allow.   The farther the network is from the individual, the deeper the fall.   A person that does not have a close or strong network may fall so far that it takes a longer time and more resources to get them back on track.   Also, when a person has a strong network they can use it to get over any obstacle that may stand in the way of achieving their goals.

<u>What is the Purpose of a Network</u>?
The purpose of a network is to:

- **Find** a job, a realtor, a girlfriend/boyfriend, a good used car at the lowest price, the best place to dine in a foreign city, the best tailor in town, a trustworthy babysitter, or the phone number to someone else in your network. Your personal network is similar to the

Internet but much more accurate and personal. You can search both the Internet and your network for things that you desire. The greatest difference between the two is when you search the internet you can get thousands of generic results from cyberspace that strangers recommend. But with your personal network you can get three to five results catered to your specific needs that people you know recommend. In addition, your personal network can call ahead to let a prospective client, hiring manager, store clerk or even a prospect for a girlfriend/boyfriend to give you a recommendation. Your personal network is the quickest and most efficient method to finding what you need. Finding something on your own versus tapping into your personal network can be paralleled to the example of waiting in a long line to purchase concert tickets versus expeditiously moving ahead due to spotting a friend at the front door and walking pass a sea of people and receiving VIP backstage passes. Your personal network helps you get what you're looking for faster and more accurately than any other means possible.

- **Develop** your career, your parenting skills, and your golf game, your ability to select a good wine, your writing skills, or just you as a person. In a strong network you will have individuals that possess a variety of skills, abilities, and talents that you can utilize to develop any

46

area of your life: personal and/or professional. Receiving advice from an individual who is doing what you envision yourself doing is priceless. Anyone at the top of their field is a product of their network. When I present workshops on relationships, I always recite the following quote by John Donne: "No man is an island." This means two things: 1) What you don't know will hurt you and 2) What you don't know someone in your network knows and knows well. Not only does your network want to support you, it needs you to stay alive and operate properly. It is the nature of a personal network to make sure that everyone in the network is prospering and developing him or herself so the bonds stay strong. Therefore, when one person does better everyone in the network benefits from the growth of that one member.

- **Support** you on your journey in life where ever it may take you personally or professionally. Your network can support you mentally, emotionally, physically, and or financially. When one member of a network is in crisis, the closest members of the network will aid that individual until they become strong enough to handle the situation themselves and move on. Without the support of the network in difficult times a person can become discouraged and lonely, as well as mentally, emotionally, physically and financially fatigued. Just like in the wild, if an animal is not with the pack it can be easy prey for a bigger, stronger animal. The support of your network can carry you through some of your most difficult and darkest times in your personal and professional life.

- **Make** you look good to prospective clients, hiring managers and or potential spouses. Have you ever hired someone or been hired for a job because of someone you know, the status of the company you used to work for, the school you attended, or maybe even because of your home town? Have you ever dated someone because of their friends or family? If so, it was because your network made you look good. Your network has the ability to make you look good or bad. Usually you choose your network or your network chooses you based on the type of person you are, so therefore, if your network looks good then you look good.

- **Be** a part of something bigger than your self; a network is an avenue to help others by using your unique skills, abilities, and talents to support their dreams through good and bad times. When you give to your network you are able to step outside of your needs and become a part of something bigger. As you give to your network, it will grow and prosper and so will you.

Who Should You Have in Your Network?

Family- Family is one of the most important parts of your network; they have known you longer and will support you quicker than anyone else in your network. But if you damage the relationship with your family, it will be more difficult to build your relationship with others in your network. Your first and closest circle in your network will most likely be your family.

Friends- Your friends are your secondary network; they are the ones that you've grown up with, played with, and even cried with. They know your strengths and weaknesses, your goals and your dreams, your failures and your victories. Your friends are the people in your network that can help you develop yourself the most. People tend to allow their friends to give them constructive criticism without defending their position.

Associates-Your associates in your network are people you know from various areas of life such as work, school, or the Parent Teacher Association meetings, for example. These relationships are not necessarily intimate or close; they may simply consist of acquaintances or individuals with whom you share interests . You may, or may not, have their telephone number but if necessary you know how to reach them. The associates in your network should know you minimally and you should be aware of their unique skills. Once you are knowledgeable of the skills in your network, you can seek opportunities to develop relationships with your associates by inviting them to a cookout/dinner party, recommending a good book that may peak interest, offering your services for free, or by simply asking about the current events surrounding their lives. Remember, associates may be distant members of the network but they can also hold the key to an opportunity of a lifetime for you or someone else in your network.

Partner-Your partners are people that believe in you, your ideas, your dreams, your goals, and they are willing to invest money, time or other resources. The partners in your network can be a family member, a friend, or even an associate that have the means to support you and believe in your cause. Partner relationships must be developed over a course of years and accrue interest equity every step of the way. It is good to have several partners in your network so you do not overwhelm or strain any one relationship.

Mentor- Your mentor is one of the most valuable, most sought-after individuals of your network. A mentor is one of the gatekeepers of success for you and your endeavors. A mentor is someone who recognizes your untapped talents, underdeveloped skills, and under-utilized abilities. They are willing to invest in the mentoring relationship and assist you in your development over the course of years. They have the experience and wisdom to help you become successful in your area of endeavor. Mentors know what you don't know, but need to know, to get to the next level in your personal and/or professional life.

In order to obtain a mentor you must seek them out and communicate your passion for what you want to do. In order to get the attention of a mentor you must first be ready and willing to follow the lead of a more experienced member of your network. Mentors are not perfect people, but they do possess the experiences, skills, and talents you need to cultivate within yourself. Because of the valuable information that you will attain in this relationship, you must be willing to be an apprentice, protégé, a personal assistant, a gofer or even wash a car or two to develop this unique relationship. To obtain a mentor you must first self examine and then conduct research on what you would like to learn and become over the next couple years. Then find a mentor that has the experience you need to help you become who you want to be. Because these individuals are highly sought after, experienced, and typically extremely busy you must know exactly what you want, have the ability to articulate what you want and, lastly, take action and be able to present your results. Mentors love to invest in people who know what they want, are not afraid to take action to get it, and can produce some level of results as a testimony to their passion for their goals and belief in self.

How do I Find a Mentor?

Good mentors are people you can find in every aspect of your life. Great places to locate a mentor include: work, school, sports clubs, bands, gospel choirs, dance classes, investment groups, health clubs, etc. To find a mentor observe individuals who are doing what you want to do and, more importantly, doing it well. Mentors love to share their wisdom and know-how with highly motivated individuals that show interest in learning from them. One of the highest forms of honor and respect a person can receive is to be asked to be a mentor. Asking someone to be a mentor says, "I value you and your experiences and I am willing to trust your judgment." Once you have identified someone who you can learn from and is also willing to teach, you have found your mentor.

Coach- Your coach is the person in your network that you compensate for their knowledge because they can show you how to move from *point A* to *point B* by using the least amount of time, money and energy. Coaches can be extremely valuable when it comes to dealing with new or unfamiliar areas of endeavor. Coaches are people that specialize in a specific area and know just about everything there is to know about becoming successful in that area. A professional coach will usually have a certification from an accredited coaching school and/or years of valuable experience in the field or area you desire to succeed in.

Coaching is partnering with clients in a thought-provoking and creative process that inspires them to maximize their personal and professional potential. Coaches encourage their clients to be themselves, to expand beyond their limitations, and become stronger human beings. Coaching is focused on providing the client with methods for focusing on self-empowerment and manifesting future goals. A coach doesn't work on healing past issues or pain. A coach offers different perspectives and works with the concept that everything the client really needs is what they already have. In a sense, the coach really acts as a mirror, but also offers questions and perspectives to get the client to think about what area of life they would like to work on.

If you want to be great, hire a coach.

How do I Find a Coach?

Before you start looking for a coach there are three questions you need to ask yourself: 1) What are my goals or what do I want to accomplish with coaching? 2) Am I open to new and different ideas of accomplishing my goals? 3) Am I committed to making my goal or dream a reality? Professional coaching costs money. You want to be sure to answer these questions truthfully so you don't waste time or money. Below are three different ways to find a professional coach:

1) The internet

You can do a search on the internet by typing in the word "coach" and the industry you want to find a coach in. For example, if you want success in your relationships you would type in "relationship coach." If you want success in marketing your business you would type in "marketing coach." If you want success in weight loss you would type in weight loss coach and so on. For every area in life you want success in, there is a coach you can hire to help you get there.

2) Word of mouth

Word of mouth is one of the best ways to find anything--especially a coach. When you get a referral from someone you know and trust, you can get specific information about the coaching services, such as style of coaching, fee, level of satisfaction/dissatisfaction, and most importantly, whether or not the coach was effective.

3) Check the industry association

Every industry has an association that offers training and in-depth information about that particular industry. The industry association will be able to guide you to the best coach that specializes in exactly what you want success in. The industry association will also have a magazine, a newsletter, and monthly meetings where you can find the industry's best.

The Mastermind Group

What is a Mastermind Group? A mastermind group is a group of two or more people that gather together once or consistently to share information with each other for the attainment of a specific goal.   Napoleon Hill, author of Think and Grow Rich, came up with the idea of a "Mastermind Alliance," which he defined as "two or more minds working actively together in perfect harmony toward a common definite objective."   This group serves as an opportunity for **like-minded** individuals to share information that will support the goals and dreams of those who participate.

There are two types of Mastermind Groups. The first type of group is where one forms a group for the sole purpose of supporting his or her goals. While the second type of group allows each person to have an opportunity to receive valuable information about how they can best achieve their goals and dreams.

Healthy Relationships vs. Unhealthy Relationships

Most people fail in building their network because they cannot tell the difference between healthy and unhealthy relationships. Unfortunately, some people do not know how to develop a healthy relationship; nor do they see the importance of distinguishing between a healthy relationship and an unhealthy relationship. The ability to develop and maintain a healthy relationship is critical and a must in order to succeed in any endeavor in life. You can always tell if a person is going to be successful by the relationships he or she is able to establish. **Healthy relationships feed you; they give you emotional nourishment.** So if a healthy relationship nourishes you emotionally, an unhealthy relationship depletes you emotionally. A lot of people are starving emotionally because of the relationships they have chosen to occupy. To get a clear understanding of a healthy and unhealthy relationship read the following definitions:

Healthy Relationships

A healthy relationship is a relationship that holds you to a higher standard than you would hold yourself. It nurtures you and inspires you to do more than you thought you could be and do more than you would do by yourself. A healthy relationship builds your character and stretches you beyond your limitations. You know you are in a healthy relationship when you feel like you are becoming a better person because of it.

Unhealthy Relationships

An unhealthy relationship is a relationship that holds you back and steals your fire and zeal for life. An unhealthy relationship will break your confidence down and have you to believe that you are of no value to the world. Unhealthy relationships can be controlling, manipulating, and extremely negative. A relationship is unhealthy when you feel like you are being drained of your energy when you are around that person.

Unfortunately, the process of getting into an unhealthy relationship is much easier than getting out of one. The first thing you need to know is that every relationship is a reflection of you. That's right. All of the relationships you have, good or bad, intimate or shallow, are a mirror of you. So, in order to change the relationships you have in your life you must change what you see in the mirror: You. As you become healthier you will encounter strife and conflict in unhealthy relationships and more intimacy in healthy relationships. The person you are participating in an unhealthy relationship with will view your growth as a threat so they will attack you; but your healthy relationships will see you as a value and seek to support you. Unhealthy relationships keep you in mental, emotional, and spiritual bondage. Unhealthy relationships also operate out of fear and are controlled by fear.

Making the Connection

Developing healthy relationships can be difficult due to a fear of meeting new people. Creating a relationship out of thin air is not only challenging, it is an art. In order to have healthy relationships in your life you must first meet people that are healthy. Since healthy people are usually engaged in personal development, as well as healthy lifestyle activities, you must become aware of the activities in your surroundings. Some activities may include personal development workshops, listening to personal development audio programs, attending health classes/fitness gym, volunteering for a worthwhile cause, attending a spiritual assembly regularly, visiting the library, going back to school to start or finish a degree, taking a cooking class, completing a highly sought after industry certification, taking a foreign language class, traveling to a foreign country, attending a local civic association meeting, taking a do-it-yourself class at the local hardware store, and so on. You are not guaranteed to find healthy people engaging in these activities, but you are more likely to find people stretching and developing themselves which will put you in the right environment to make the connection with the right people.

If you want to meet someone different then do something different.

The following are three different ways to meet people when you are engaging in healthy, growth-oriented activities:

The direct approach
The direct approach to making a connection is walking right up to a person and asking them their name, telling them yours, and starting a conversation. This usually works well for people that are extroverts and who enjoy meeting new people. This also may be the best approach if you know exactly who you want to talk to and why.

<u>The soft approach</u>

The soft approach is used to soften a meeting between two people. In other words, the soft approach makes it easier to start a conversation between you and a total stranger. To use this approach you will find something you share in common with the other person. The conversation should start off with a comment, a question, or a compliment.

A **comment** could be:

- "It looks like rain."
- "This is a great day for a drive"
- "This traffic should be dying down soon."

Make sure your comment is somewhat positive and light so the conversation starts on a good note.

A **question** could be:

- "What type of work do you do?"
- "How is the weather outside?"
- "How did you like the food at that restaurant?"
- "How do you like your car?"
- "Is that book a good read?"

Questions are great conversation starters. These questions can come from something visual and/or obvious so you do not make the other person, or yourself, feel uncomfortable.

59

A **compliment** could be:

- "I love those shoes."

- "I like your watch."

- "Who does your hair?"

- "That is a nice computer."

- "I have always admired that car. How does it drive?"

- "That is a really nice suit"

Paying someone a compliment is sure to get the desired response. Compliments are great because they make you and the other person relaxed and everyone loves to receive compliments as long as they are genuine. Compliments can lead a conversation in the right direction, as well as, create an instant attraction to you, the compliment giver.

The third-party approach

The third party approach occurs when someone introduces you to someone else. They will usually state your name, occupation, and share some background information (if they know it). This is one of the most common ways of meeting people, especially individuals of particular importance (i.e., president of a large company, a government official, a media figure, a well known author, or a sports icon). When you are introduced to another person by a mutual contact you immediately gain credibility. It is like a loan and you are borrowing the credit of someone else until you have your own.

This is also a great way to make the connection because you do not have to figure out how to begin conversing, it is already initiated for you. All you have to do is allow your greatness to shine.

Teamwork Makes the Dream Work

No man is an island, this means no man or woman can achieve their goals and dreams by themselves. It takes a team to make your dream work. Whether we are talking about the 44th President of the United States, Barack Obama; world renowned talk show host Oprah Winfrey; the inventor of the light bulb, Thomas Edison; former president of General Electric, Jack Welch; or championship basketball player, Michael Jordan, a team is an integral part of manifesting your dreams into reality.

People destined for greatness don't allow just anyone on their team; they look for people with character and leadership abilities as well as individuals who can help them become a better person and catapult them into Greatness.

Here are Some Questions to Ask Yourself to Help You Build Your Network:

1. Who are the five closest people to you in your network?

_____

_____

2. Are the people closest to you in your network consciously helping you to become a better person or even a great person?

_____

_____

3. Do the five closest people in your network know about your goals and dreams and do they believe in you?

_____

_____

4. Who are the members of your network you have unhealthy relationships with? How much time are you spending with those members?

_____

_____

5. Do you have a coach and a mentor in your network? If not, why?

_____

_____

6. In the past 30 days, how many people have you talked

to in your network besides your top closest five?

_____

_____

7. In the past 30 days, how many people have you exchanged contact information with?

_____

_____

8. In the past 30 days, how many people have you
followed up with after you exchanged contact
information?

_____

_____

9. In the last past 30 days, how many people in your
network have you helped with their goals and dreams?

_____

_____

10. What are the names of five people that you would like to
meet that could help you achieve your goals and
dreams? Why haven't you met them yet?

_____

_____

11. What types of people do you need in your network to make you great?

_____

_____

12. What can you do to develop your network?

_____

_____

13. What type of person would you need to become to attract the people you want to be in your network?

_____

_____

The Seeds of Action

1. Call the top five people in your network and ask them what are their current goals and dreams. Then ask them what you can do to help them achieve their goals and dreams. After you have called your top five, call one person out of your network every week to find out how you can support their goals and dreams.

2. Find at least one networking event or networking opportunity per month such as personal development workshops/training, attending health classes/fitness

gym, volunteering for a local non-profit, attending a spiritual assembly regularly, visiting the library, sign up for a special interest class like cooking, foreign language, traveling, attending a local civic association meeting, take a *do-it-yourself* class at the local hardware store or check the local cafés, local library, newspapers, internet/social networking sites like Facebook and Twitter, and your personal network for local networking events.

3. When you receive a networking contact follow up within a week or two at the latest.

4. Take as many personal development and professional development training classes as you can afford both financially and time wise.

5. Read a book that emphasizes the importance of networking, personal energy, social intelligence, and or emotional intelligence to help you become a better networker.

6. Take a member of your network or a "people person" with you when you decide to attend a networking event, especially if you struggle with networking.

7. Set a goal to become a better networker.

8. Start a Mastermind Group.

9. Share this networking information with a friend.

The Seed of Tenacity

"Tenacity is the ability to hold on until the ride is over."

The Gum Under Your Shoes

Have you ever been walking down the sidewalk and noticed that you stepped on a wad of gum, and then tried to remove it from your shoe? After an hour of trying to remove it, you realize that this gum is there to stay until it is ready to be removed. This is the essence of tenacity.

Tenacity is the ability to holdfast, to be retentive, not to be easily pulled apart from a desired outcome. It is one of the major deciding factors in your ability to become great. Average people give up relatively easy when they cannot achieve their goals\pursuits in a short period of time. Prematurely giving up leads to people becoming beaten by life. Because people are "creatures of habit" most of our actions are routine, especially our tolerance for mental endurance. To have mental endurance a person must exercise their mind. They have to push and sometimes extend their mind beyond the imaginable to obtain a desired outcome. In the intro of this book it was noted that people who are willing to sacrifice always get what they really want out of life. To have tenacity is to have an unwavering mind to obtain a desired outcome at almost any cost.

Never Give Up Unless You Need to

"Never give up" is a motto of most high achievers. What they don't tell you is what they had to give up to accomplish their goals. If you never give up on anything, you will be stuck spending your time trying to accomplish unsuitable and unworthy tasks that do not serve your greatness. To give up on an unworthy goal is to make room for a greater and more feasible goal. For example, if you want to lose 20 pounds but your schedule will not permit it because of other pursuits such as a book club meeting, working late, watching television, checking e-mails, etc. you will have to prioritize your activities based on importance. The value of a goal or dream can help you decide which to pursue first. To accomplish your goals and dreams it will take a lot of energy and for the really big ones it will take your life. So when you make a decision to set a goal or chase a dream, make sure you are ready to pay the price of tenacity.

Here are Some Questions to Help You Increase Your Tenacity:

1. What is your level of tenacity on a scale of 1 to 5 with 1 being the highest and 5 being the lowest?

_____

_____

2. How long does it take before you give up on a task or a goal?

   _____

   _____

3. List all of your accomplishments that took a great deal of tenacity to achieve?

   _____

   _____

4. Who is the person in your life that possesses the greatest level of tenacity?

   _____

   _____

5. Do you have any tasks or goals that you need to give up in order to make room for a greater goal or dream?

   _____

   _____

The Seeds of Action

1. Take time to identify a task that you have been trying to accomplish but never had the tenacity to stick it out.

2. Turn your task into a goal if it is not already one by giving it a deadline and doing research. See the <u>Seeds of a Goal</u> chapter for more information on goal setting.

3. Sit down in a quiet room and write this goal on a piece of paper; then think of how you will accomplish it. Think of the obstacles that usually get in your way. On the other side of the paper write down each obstacle that is in the way of accomplishing your goal. Next to each obstacle come up with a solution you can realistically carry out.

4. Take action on achieving your goal and sticking to it until it's done.

5. You may also want to get a mentor or hire a life coach to assist you on staying focused and persistent. See the <u>Seeds of a Network</u> chapter for more information on Life Coaches and mentors.

6. Make sure you stay motivated. You can do this by creating a dream board, listening to motivational and inspirational CD programs as well as thinking about how great you will feel when you have accomplished your goal.

The Seed of Money

"Money is a symbol of consciousness"

What is the Purpose of Money?

Money was originally used for paying debt. But, because people have abused it, money has put people in debt. Originally, money, also known as legal tender, started out as an I.O.U. and as a form of payment for work done or goods received. Now, it is used for the fortunate to perpetuate wealth while the less fortunate are debt ridden by capital savvy individuals that know how to manipulate financial systems. Simply put, money is nothing other than a symbol of value. The key word is *symbol*.

How to Attract Money?

Average people work for money while others spend their lives chasing it. Money finds people who are destined for greatness. Money needs something to connect to so it seeks its equal or greater value. Anything of an equal or greater value it follows, anything with a lesser value it repels. This is the concept of the *money magnet*. How does one become a money magnet? First, you must distinguish the slave from the master. Money is the slave and you are the master. Most average people behave as if it is the other way around. Why is this so? Individuals are conditioned at an early age to chase money. Keep in mind you only chase what you think you can't have. Generally, people suppose they do not have enough money so they start chasing it, but it never fails. Just when they think they are going to get enough money, it eludes them. Chasing money is just like trying to get to the end of a rainbow; the closer you get the farther away it appears. This occurs because money follows people who believe that they already have it. When you stress about money your body becomes rigid, your breathing becomes shallow, you get headaches, and your creative thinking becomes stagnant. For the average person this way of thinking is a way of life.

If you want to become a money magnet you must think like one. In your mind you must believe that money wants you. You must believe that no matter what financial situation you find yourself in money is on its way to you. When you are feeling stressed over money repeat this affirmation in your mind or aloud, *"I have everything I need, therefore, I need nothing."* This is a very powerful statement and can change your concept of money. For this to truly be a part of your life you must exercise faith. Faith is believing in what you cannot see. For more information on faith see the <u>Seeds of Faith</u> chapter.

Money is Like Oxygen

Money ranks up there with oxygen; you don't think about it until you need it. And just like you have to release carbon dioxide in order to receive oxygen, you must also give money in order to receive it. Once you stop giving carbon dioxide and receiving oxygen you die. The same is true with money; once you stop giving it and receiving it you become financially dead. When you do not release money you impede the flow of money to you. When you give you act as an artery in the **Universal Eco System**. That **Universal Eco System** is what keeps the United States economy alive. It is the financial circulatory system that allows money to flow to and from one person or entity to another person or entity.

Imagine walking to your car one morning and realizing it will not start. So you call a tow truck, which costs money, and then the repair shop says you need a new engine. You are so mad that you could kick anything you won't break your foot on. Out of frustration you ask yourself, "Why me, why did this have to happen to me? Every time I get some extra money I have to give it away." A couple of things to point out here, 1) your stress and rigidity will repel any money that would have been coming your way. This is also called **spiritual blockage**. 2) You are missing the bigger picture. Did you consider that the tow truck driver or the repair shop owner needed your money? They are a part of the **Universal ECO System** just like you.

Their belief or faith has allowed unforeseen situations to occur that give you an opportunity to financially exhale and make way for you to inhale. When you do not accept this opportunity to exhale you also forfeit your opportunity to inhale or receive financial benefits. Think about this: every best selling book written on success or on how to get rich has at least one chapter on giving. Whether you call it tithing, community support, or paying it forward, it is a process of supporting a greater purpose than your own existence. Do you see that by not holding back your giving you become a part of something greater than you? You become part of a system that allows everyone who believes in it to get their needs met? So next time you have to pay a bill or someone you owe money just know that you are freeing up room to receive something greater.

How to Use Money

Money should be used as a tool for several purposes. The following is a list of the three main things money should be used for:

1. Sustaining your lifestyle
2. Investing in projects that can enhance society
3. Giving to the church, or community programs or individuals who seek an opportunity to advance in life

The following list is three things money should not be used for:

1. Gambling

2. Purchasing material items solely for status and self indulgence

3. Putting others that are less fortunate and less knowledgeable of money in financial bondage

Here are Some Questions to Ask Yourself About Money:

1. Are you in debt? If so, why? Be sure to list *reasons* NOT *excuses.*

_____

_____

2. Rate yourself as a money manager on a scale of 1 to 5, 1 being the lowest and 5 being the highest.

_____

_____

3. Does money work for you or do you work for money?

_____

_____

4. Do you get upset when you have to pay a bill or when something unexpected comes up?

_____

_____

5. How often do you give money to less fortunate individuals, churches, community programs, or worthwhile projects?

_____

_____

6. Do you invest your money? If not, why not? Make sure to list reasons, not excuses.

_____

_____

7. Do you save any money out of each paycheck? If not, why not? Make sure to list reasons, not excuses?

_____

_____

8. What have you done to educate yourself on how to properly use money?

_____

_____

The Seeds of Action

1. Create a budget that includes giving, saving, and investing.

2. Take a financial literacy class.

3. Hire a financial adviser.

4. Make a habit of giving money to people and or projects that you would normally not give to.

5. Read a book on the power of giving

6. Talk to someone who is a giver in your network about how to start giving back or tithing.

7. Start looking at money like oxygen and every time you receive make sure you give.

8. Set a goal to allow yourself to become a part of the Universal Eco System

The Seed of Faith

"Today I will walk by faith not by sight."

What is Faith?

Faith is the ability to believe in what you cannot see. It is trusting in something other than your ability to handle a situation. To trust is to surrender mental, physical, and spiritual control of a matter that is beyond your conscious level of awareness. Often times the words *belief* and *faith* are used interchangeably. Here's the difference between *belief* and *faith*: belief is trusting in something you can see or have experienced before, while faith is trusting in something you have never seen or experienced before. Ultimately, faith is letting go of something you know for something greater. The "something greater" you will receive is awareness of the greatness that already lives inside of you; it is waiting to be discovered.

How Does Faith Work?

Faith is not a thought, a saying, or a scripture in a religious book. Faith is a verb. Faith is an action! It is how you live your life. For example, do you think before you sit in a chair that you have sat in before? Why not? It's because you **believe** the chair will hold you and not allow you to hit the ground. This is what I call a belief. You see the chair; it appears sturdy; you've sat in it before so you have reference points making you believe the chair will hold you. On the other hand, if you've never been skydiving you may think of all of the possibilities or outcomes that could happen. In this situation, it may be difficult for most people to believe something less than favorable will happen; however, it is faith that allows the novice skydiver to take the plunge. These two examples are extreme so let's take a look at *everyday* faith in action. There are several daily activities that require a certain level of faith in order to engage in them. Some of these activities include the following:

- Tithing to a church
- Giving money to a homeless person
- Asking your boss for a raise when you have only been employed 18 months and no one in your department has ever received a raise
- Listening to your spouse about how to deal with one of your character flaws
- Giving your teenage daughter your car to go out on a Saturday night
- Joining a multi-level marketing company to pay off some credit card debt
- Riding a roller coaster for the first time
- Public speaking
- Asking someone you admire out on a date
- Asking for help from someone that you believe dislikes you

- Telling the truth about yourself
- Investing in stock

These are just some activities that require some level of faith in our day-to-day lives.

Remember, faith is an action!

People with little or no faith usually do not make it a habit to try new activities such as eating different types of food, going on adventurous outings and meeting new people. In order to have faith, you must be open for new and sometimes uncomfortable experiences.

Let's use the example of giving a homeless person some money. This is a very common act that takes a little faith. Belief is giving a homeless person money and you know that they are going to buy food with it because you have seen them do it before. But having faith is giving the homeless money and not being concerned with the outcome. Faith comes in when you let go of the outcome, because you know it is not in your hands. The main reason why most people have a hard time using faith is because they want to be able to control the outcome. **Not knowing the outcome is where you grow, it is how you become closer to God.** To be close to God is to know that His wisdom and favor is working in every situation no matter if the outcome is favorable or unfavorable. Think about it. You learn from unfavorable situations more than you learn from favorable situations. So as you use your faith, you grow and gain closeness to God and ultimately become free and detached from the outcome of any situation.

Where does stress come from? Stress comes from worrying over the outcome of a situation. Individuals stress over situations because they desire control over the outcome. If you knew that every situation that occurred in your life would have a favorable outcome, then you would be less stressed and essentially free of worry. Here is a very important question pertaining to faith: What makes the outcome to a situation favorable or unfavorable? The answer and common denominator to every situation is _**you**_. You decide what is favorable and what is unfavorable. If you decided that every situation, no matter what the outcome, was favorable in your eyes because you learn and you grow from it, then you become _**free**_. To walk in faith, is to be without worry; it is the ability to allow your self to let go of the outcome and _**be free**_. To be free is to be happy and unencumbered to access your greatness.

Here are Some Questions to Ask to Begin Planting the Seed of Faith:

1. Rate how often you worry on a scale from 1 to 5, 1 being the lowest and 5 being the highest. Take time to think about your answer to this question since worrying is such an integrated part of our everyday lives. We are

sometimes unaware of how much time we spend worrying.

_____

_____

3. Do you have a problem with trusting people or situations you do not know?

_____

_____

4. Do you like trying new things? If not, why not?

_____

_____

5. Do you like meeting new people? If not, why not?

_____

_____

6. Are you uncomfortable when you are unsure of the outcome to a situation?

_____

_____

7. Do you try to control the outcome of situations in your life? If so, why?

    _____

    _____

8. Who in your life would you consider a person that walks by faith? Why?

    _____

    _____

The Seeds of Action

1. Create a list of 5 recent situations where you have walked by faith and then create a list of 5 recent situations where you have not walked by faith. Study both lists to determine how you can increase your faith.
2. Find a mentor or hire a life coach to help you increase your faith. For more information on mentors and life coaches see the Seeds of a Network chapter.
3. Join a church or religious institution that will support the development of your faith.
4. Every morning repeat this affirmation to yourself: *"I do not need to be in control; therefore I will be obedient to what God wants for me and for my life. Every situation I encounter is for my good, no matter what the outcome is; I am enough to handle*

every situation that comes my way because God watches over me. And because of this, today I am Free."

The Seed of Listening

"Listen to understand"

Great People Know How to Listen

Listening is one of the attributes of great people. The ability to listen is a skill that can change your life in a matter of minutes. To listen is to be present in the *now* and in the *know*. To listen is to seek information outside of yourself and to be an observer of life so that you can live more abundantly. Listening is how you achieve new information orally, visually, cognitively, and spiritually.

Average people listen to what others have to say…sometimes; great people listen to what life has to say… most times.

What are You Listening for?

In communication, people usually hear and view information through a filter. This filter is made up of our beliefs, experiences, and viewpoints. So, when we receive new information we unconsciously compare it to our beliefs, experiences, and perspectives.

Our beliefs or vantage point are what we know to be true; our experiences are the situations that we have been through; and our viewpoint is our position. For example, you believe that your supervisor is treating you unfairly. Three months later you are promoted to supervisor and now one of your employees think you are treating him/her unfairly. In the example, your viewpoint changed when your position changed. No longer are you in the position of a staff member, instead you have repositioned yourself as a supervisor with different duties and responsibilities. Therefore, because your experience is different, your beliefs (what you know) have changed. You have a new perspective from your promotion, but because you were once a staff member you can now relate to how your staff feel. Your ability to listen in each of these situations is based on position. Changing your position in any situation can help you listen for the solution to any problem.

In life, people who are destined for greatness make a conscious decision to start listening to what life has to tell them. Life is your teacher. If you do not listen to each situation, favorable or unfavorable, you will not pass the test. That's right; each situation that you go through is a test! Average people simply go through situations, but great people *grow through* situations. Average people ask themselves, "Why did I have to go through this situation?" People destined for greatness ask, "What can I learn from this situation?" Each unfavorable situation you encounter possesses valuable information that can aid you as you move toward your greatness.

Remember: Unfavorable situations teach you what does not work, favorable situations teach you what does work. If you find yourself going through more unfavorable situations than favorable, stop and ask yourself, "What am I doing to place me in these situations?" and "What can I learn from it?" The situations you want to listen most intensely are those that keep reoccurring. Those reoccurring situations are the ones that are trying to teach you something.

Listening to Your Inner Self

Your inner self is what some people call your intuition, your higher nature, or the God within. For the sake of this book, I will call it your inner self. The inner self is your authentic self; the "you" you were born to be. It is the greatness within. Your inner self operates similarly to a global positioning system (GPS) or a navigational system. It lets you know when you are off course or going the wrong way. The problem with most people's GPS is that it is turned down.

One of the first words children learn to speak is "no" because they have heard it repeatedly from their parents. Parents, teachers, and other authority figures commonly tell us, "You can do anything you put your mind to" while simultaneously saying, "no" and "can't". Unintentionally, the people in our lives turn down our internal GPS to protect us from harm; however, we tend to lose our way to our greatness and purpose in life due to fear.

In order to turn up your GPS practice meditation and prayer for guidance and direction. To hear your inner GPS you must turn down other noises in your life such as unhealthy relationships, trashy television, loud and abrasive music filled with profanity, reading junk e-mails, advice from too many people at one time, and noisy ring tones on your cell phone. To listen to your inner self you must be in tune with the real you. At first the inner self will whisper until you know what it sounds like; and then it will sing, for it has been waiting for someone to listen to it. It has been waiting to tell you *about your greatness within!*

<u>Here are Some Questions to Ask Yourself to Increase</u>
<u>Your Ability to Listen</u>:

1. What is life telling you?

_____

_____

2. Have you ever repeated a similar unfavorable situation?

_____

_____

3. What are five things that you have learned from the last unfavorable situation?

_____

_____

4. What are five things that you have learned from the last favorable situation?

_____

_____

5. Have you ever been given good advice on a situation and chose not to listen? If so, why?

_____

_____

6. What unfavorable situations continually repeat themselves in your life? These unfavorable situations can be in the areas of finances, relationships, health, education, career development, and so on.

_____

_____

7. How can you reposition yourself to change your experiences and beliefs in order to succeed on your

journey to greatness?

_____

_____

The Seed of Action

1. Think about the last situation that caused you the most stress and write it down on a piece of paper.

2. Write five things you can learn from this situation.

3. Find someone who has previously gone through a similar situation but is now successful. Find out how they overcame their obstacles to achieve success. For more information on finding people to help you overcome your obstacles see the Seed of a Network chapter.

4. To mentally change your position without making physical changes, interview everyone involved in the situation and put yourself in their shoes. This will require that you have to mentally experience what the other people have experienced. When you ask them questions refrain from being defensive, practice being open to their experience and perspective. Being open is a skill that takes practice to master but over time will

tremendously springboard your growth towards greatness.

5. Practice listening to what life has to say by journaling. Write down each epiphany or "a ha" moment. It is in those moments that life speaks to you.

6. What is your inner self telling you to do at work, at school, in your relationship, at home and with your finances?

The Seed of Leadership

"Leaders are not born; they are people who have made a decision to step into their greatness."

Everyone is a Leader at Some Point in Their Life

If you have ever led a sports team, a class project, a department at work, a small group, or a child across the street, then you are a leader.

Most people don't view themselves as leaders, despite having innate abilities to do so. As a result, most people do not act like leaders or place themselves in leadership positions. Becoming a leader is a decision that you make when you realize that your actions affect more than just you. When you decide to step up to the plate and take responsibility for your actions, you become more aware of what you do and why you do it. In order to become a leader one must become conscious of their actions and thoughts and how it impacts your direction in life. When a person travels this road they consciously travel the high and narrow road, the road filled with obstacles, fear, self-doubt, admiration, and a sense of self-accomplishment but most of all, it is an internal journey to finding your greatness.

When you decide to become a leader, not only does it bring out the best in others, but it ultimately brings out the best in you.

Leaders are Project-Oriented

Leaders are people who see that something needs to be done and they take action to make it happen. These individuals usually work well on projects of various sizes. No matter the size of the task, a leader will jump in with both feet and ready to work. True leaders rarely have a problem finding employment or others that will support their dreams and goals. Great leaders are sought after because of the lack of people willing to take responsibility.

Time Management

Leaders keep track of time and manage it based on the projects they are working on. Leaders do not only see the value in time, they are always seeking new tools and techniques to leverage it in their favor. Leaders know that time is the one commodity you cannot purchase, you cannot trade, and you definitely cannot find it on *eBay*. It is the most valuable commodity any person can control. Once your time is up, so is your work here on this earth; therefore, real leaders spend their time wisely.

Leaders are Committed

Leaders are committed to outcomes, especially during hard times. They are strong-willed individuals that will see a project or situation through no matter what, come hell or high water. Leaders are visionaries who can see the harvest even before the seeds have been planted. When a true leader decides to commit to the completion of a task, their commitment is not only to others but also to themselves–ultimately, leaders hold themselves accountable.

Leaders Make Things Happen

Leaders know how to make things happen. They possess extreme ingenuity. They are analytical and methodical thinkers. They plan well in advance for what could go wrong and even for what should never go wrong.

Leaders Develop Other Leaders

Leaders take the time to invest in other leaders. They see the potential in others and do their best to develop it. Leaders are always searching for protégés and predecessors for future projects and to assist with large projects. To develop another leader you must first work to develop yourself into a great leader. Great leaders know how to harness their own potential by seeking counsel through other leaders. If you are a true leader, other leaders will be drawn to you so that they may share in your wisdom.

Leaders Know How to Communicate Their Vision

Leaders are communicators who not only talk about a dream but also show you the dream through their words. Great leaders are always studying so they can better communicate the understanding of their vision. Great leaders have the ability to appeal to not only people's minds but to their hearts as well. When great leaders speak, people listen and take action.

Leaders Lead by Example

Leaders are models and coaches. They show you what they want you to do by leading the way with their own actions. Leaders make a habit out of doing what is necessary, not for the success of themselves but for the success of their followers.

Leaders Possess Courage

Courage is the one common denominator all leaders must possess! It is a secret ingredient that helps leaders rise to the top. Courage is not the absence of fear; it is taking action in spite of fear. Courage kicks in when you realize that something must be done and you are the only one willing to pay the price of making it happen.

Leaders Leave a Legacy

From the beginning of time, leaders have been studied for the gems of information imbedded within their legacy. A leader's legacy is the grade he receives when he has finished his job here on earth. A leader's character illuminates his or her legacy so that those who come behind him/her trust in it and is enriched by it. Your legacy will prove to those who do not know you what is possible for them in their lives. Ultimately, what you do today will light the path for others to follow tomorrow.

Here are Some Questions to Ask in Order to Develop the Leader Within:

1. Do you consider yourself a leader? Why or why not?

   _____

   _____

2. Do you have any followers?

   _____

   _____

3. What leaders do you admire the most and why?

   _____

   _____

4. What was the last project or activity you took the lead on without anyone asking you to do so?

   _____

   _____

5. What leadership skills and qualities do you possess?

What leadership skills and qualities would you like to develop?

_____

_____

6. Identify the leaders at work, school, on the team, in your family and among your friends. What have you learned from them?

_____

_____

The Seeds of Action

1. Take at least three different classes on management and leadership.
2. Find a leader to mentor you. See the Seeds of a Network chapter for more information on mentors.
3. Read at least two different books on leadership.
4. Read at least two different books on management.
5. Find work, school, or community projects you have the skills and ability to lead and step into your greatness.

The Seed of Service

"Service is the price you pay for Greatness"

Great People Make a Habit of Serving Others

From Martin Luther King, Jr. to President Barack Obama, from Mahatma Gandhi to Mother Teresa great people make a decision to serve, not because they want to be great, but because they feel a great obligation to give back to their communities. Great people know that service is necessary in order for others to have an opportunity at life.

People Remember What You Do for Others More Than What You Do for Yourself

At the end of your life the only thing people will remember is your unpaid debt and the good deeds you have done for others. When you have found a strong reason to live you become immune to the fear of death, therefore you focus your time and energy on making your life count.

Spend Your Life Giving Away Your Innate Talents

Imagine being present outside your body in the room as you take your last breath. Then imagine all the books you said you would write, the artwork you told yourself you would create, the poems you didn't have time to write, the non-profit you promised you would start, the degree you said you would finish, the movie you said you would write, the marathon you said you would run, the relationship you said you would mend but you never took time to do it. And now you don't have the time to do anything. How many people do you think will miss out on your service to the world?

Service is more than giving your time; it is giving your talents. Service is to give away the very gift that you have been given by the creator.

The Three Pillars of Service

1. **Attitude**

   If you are to render service to anyone you have to have an attitude of service. Your attitude is your mental position or feeling about giving. If you feel like you are losing something when you give, you will need to reverse your thinking or your attitude about giving. Look at it this way: if your hand is closed you may be able to keep what you have, but you definitely would not be able to receive anything new. In other words, to give is to receive. To serve you must cultivate an attitude of giving and know that giving begets receiving.

2. **Authenticity**

   If you are to serve you should not do it because you have to, you should do it because you deeply

feel it is necessary and it is something you strongly believe in. If you serve solely with the intention of giving to get or because someone makes you feel guilty, your service will be short lived and others will perceive you as lacking in authenticity and they will not believe in you or your project/cause.

3. **Meeting the needs of others**

   When you serve you should know what is needed and try to meet that need. If you see a person's leg is broken, don't put a band-aid on their leg. In other words, put energy into fixing the problem, not the symptom. When you are able to meet the needs of others not only does the receiving party greatly benefit, but you as the giver receive something that money can't buy: a sense of self worth and intrinsic value.

<u>External and Internal Customer Service</u>

Most companies believe that customer service is a vital part of their success and their long-term financial vitality. But what some companies seem to overlook too often is that there are two types of customer service. The first type of customer service is external customer service, the most commonly promoted and written about form of customer service. This type of service is when you or your company serves another person or company that is outside of your day-to-day surrounding, such as clients and people you do not necessarily know intimately or personally. The second type of service is the most important and it is the most overlooked, as well as, the hardest to deliver. It is internal customer service and it is the highest level of service a person can give. Internal customer service reveals your character. Your character is who you really are when no one else is looking. Internal customer service is when you serve the people in your immediate environment, such as the people you work with, your wife, your husband, your children, close friends, and any other intimate relationships you have. This is the most important type of service because these people are the people that support you, your projects, your causes, your dreams, and even other relationships you are involved with. Your ability to effectively serve your internal customers will foster your personal success in life and ultimately pave the road to greatness.

Service is the doorway to greatness and it is up to you to walk through the door.

<u>Here are Some Questions to Ask Yourself to Increase Your Ability to Serve Others</u>:
1. In the last 30 days how much time have you spent serving others?

_____

_____

2. In the last 30 days who has rendered service to you?

_____

_____

3. Who are the people in your life you admire that serve others on a regular basis?

_____

_____

4. What are 6 different ways you could serve others at work, at home, or in your community?

_____

_____

5. What type of organization are you most likely to volunteer your services and why?

_____

_____

6. Have you ever thought about becoming a mentor? If not, why?

_____

_____

7. Have you ever been mentored and what did you gain from it?

_____

_____

8. How do you feel when you give your time, your money and your energy to someone or a worthwhile cause?

_____

_____

9. How can you start implementing better external and internal customer service?

_____

_____

10. Are you willing to commit to serving others without receiving an immediate return?

_____

_____

The Seeds of Action

1. Create a plan to serve others. This plan should include, the names of people, organizations, and the

causes you are interested in serving as well as deadlines for when you will do so.

2. Everyday find small ways of serving others.

3. **Ask the people in your immediate environment, such as the people you work with, your family members, and close friends how you could better serve them.**

4. Watch or read a biography about someone who has committed their life to serving others, such as Martin Luther King, Jr., President Barack Obama, Mahatma Gandhi, the Dalai Lama, Mother Teresa, or Jesus.

5. Start a service journal to write down information about your service projects, the progress of your cause, and the difference you have made in the lives of others. By creating a journal you can reflect on your experiences and the benefits you have provided for others and your community. Your journal will be your gift to yourself for serving. Take time to look at it when you need cheering up or a boost of self-confidence.

The Seed of Forgiveness

"Forgiveness releases you, not the other person"

What is the Purpose of Forgiveness?

Forgiveness is a tool that can be used to bring forth peace, happiness and greatness. To have the ability to forgive is to have the ability to live and to transcend life's greatest obstacle: the fear of letting go. Forgiveness teaches people to get over themselves and become bigger. When a person becomes bigger they have the capacity to give more because they have become more. They have become bigger in their sense of who they are and their internal wealth. Forgiveness makes happiness possible and greatness obtainable.

Forgiveness is another way of saying, "I release you from your debt; I no longer need you to pay for what you have done to me." **When you are able to forgive a person, you are able to refocus your emotional energy on whatever matters most in your life, whatever you want to grow in your life, and whatever you want to create in your life such as peace, happiness, love, and/or wealth**.

A person cannot truly become great without practicing forgiveness. Holding on to past debt will emotionally weigh you down and steal the joy from your life experience. The main purpose for forgiveness is to free yourself, not the other person.

<u>Emotional Chips</u>

Imagine sitting at a poker table and you only have $100 to play with. You would think twice about placing a bet or you may not even bet at all, especially if the average bet is $25 or $50. Now, imagine sitting at a poker table with $1,000. You may bet a little more often because you have more chips to bet. The poker chips are similar to emotional chips. Emotional chips are your emotional energy and you can decide to spend them on anything you want, good or bad. When you decide to spend your emotional chips on past debts, you give your energy and your value away. But when you spend it on experiences that enhance your life, such as a healthy relationship, your favorite hobby, taking a class to learn something new, or even just taking time out to focus on yourself, your emotional chips will start to increase by leaps and bounds.

Most people do not take risks in life because they do not have enough emotional chips to play. This is because most of their emotional chips are tied up or invested in past hurts and offenses.

When you start to forgive people for their debts, especially the ones you know you will never be paid back for, you have more emotional chips in your account to play with and your life's energy will start to increase dramatically. This means you will have the freedom to give the emotional chips to things that make you happy and that will benefit your life and the life of others now and in the future.

The Healing Power of Forgiveness

Letting go of past debt will not only free you up, but it can also heal you.

"Recent studies have shown that practicing forgiveness can have a positive effect on our health. According to a study at Duke University Medical Center, people who have forgiven others experience lower levels of physical pain, anger, and depression. In the study, people with chronic back pain felt less pain and anxiety when they used meditation to help them forgive and release their anger.

Forgiveness may also benefit your heart. Researchers at the University of Tennessee have found a connection between being forgiving, blood pressure and stress. According to the study, people who forgave more easily had a lower resting blood pressure and heart rate than people who did not forgive as easily. In addition, people who were rated as "high forgivers" were more likely to work harder to resolve conflict. As a result, they also tended to have stronger relationships.

Forgiveness is also healing. Research suggests that the ability to forgive yourself and others can boost your

107

immune system and help you to recover more quickly from illness or disease. Holding a grudge is like putting your body through a major stressful event. Your blood pressure rises, your muscles tense, and you sweat more. When you forgive the grudge, your body can relax and release the stress.

Forgiveness may be healing because it is an antidote to anger, which has been shown to be detrimental to your health. A study in a recent issue of *Neurology* has found that anger and negative emotions can precede a stroke. In the study, people who had strokes were more likely to experience feelings of anger within the two hours prior to the stroke. In addition to the physical benefits, letting go of anger by practicing forgiveness can enrich your relationships and ultimately help you to be a happier person."

Source: www.healthandgoodness.com
Written by: Minh Nguyen

The Road to Forgiveness

The road to forgiveness is an internal journey to find peace, happiness and fulfillment in life. **Life is the ultimate journey of self-mastery; if you can master yourself then you don't feel the need to master anyone else.** The road to forgiveness starts with you and ends with you. You are responsible for charting the course, navigating the course, and staying the course. Everyone's road will be different based on past experiences, temperament, character, and inspiration to let go. Along your road, you will encounter peaks, valleys, dark tunnels, broken bridges, treacherous cliffs, open fields and long stretches. Do not avoid but embrace every problem and obstacle that finds you, because it is there to prepare you for the next one ahead.

As you travel your road to forgiveness learn from the past, hope for the future, and live in the present.

Releasing the Brakes

Have you ever jumped in your car, started it up, and stepped on the gas only to realize you forgot to release the parking brakes? Forgiveness is your parking brake and if you truly want to move forward in life you must decide to let go.

It is time to let go and renew yourself. It is time to let go of the past, embrace the present and create the future. Open up your heart, free your mind, and start living your life the way it was meant to be lived. **Only you can control your destiny; only you can release your brakes; only you can give yourself permission to move forward in life.** So, let go of the hurt you know and allow life to carry you beyond your fear to the endless possibility of greatness that lives within you.

Who Should You Forgive First?

Have you tried to forgive someone for something they did to you only to later learn you never really forgave that person?

This happens because most of the time the person you are trying to forgive is only a reflection of past hurts from your childhood or young adult life. The stages of childhood and young adulthood are highly impressionable periods of development because it is the time when you are unconsciously forming your own personal beliefs and values that will govern your most intimate relationships. This is also the time when you are most vulnerable and susceptible to trauma.

So in order to fully forgive you must forgive the first person you recall who made you feel hurt in that particular area of life. In order to do this you must do some soul searching. In most cases it may be someone close to you such as a caretaker (i.e., father, mother, brother, sister, grandfather, grandmother, stepfather, stepmother, coach, teacher).

Most of the people with whom you start the forgiveness process will not be conscious that they need forgiving. Just remember that forgiving is not about the other person, it is about you and your healing; the other person just gets a bonus. Also keep in mind that as you forgive people for what you believe was an offense, your relationships will automatically become healthier and more intimate.

Six Steps to Forgive

1. Identify the person you want to forgive.

2. Understand this is about you not them, you are really releasing yourself not them.

3. Write down the offense no matter how small or big.

4. Write a positive outcome you experienced from the offense. What did you learn about you (not the offense)?

5. Put yourself in their shoes. Hurt people, hurt other people so if this person hurt you, who hurt them? This may be difficult because most people cannot get beyond themselves to feel someone else's pain that offended them, but this is how you grow in life. You may feel apprehensive about this, but this is a part of the journey to forgiveness. If they are still living you can ask them some questions about their childhood or young adult life. If they are deceased, you can do research by asking family members or assume what might have happened. Just remember, people usually give what they have not what you think they should have.

6. To complete the process, have an open dialogue with the person that committed the offense, or an objective person, to discuss why you are not offended anymore and why you wanted to forgive them in the first place. Your "why" is very important because it shows others, as well as yourself, the reason you let go. If your reason is not authentic, the person you share with and the person you forgive will know. More importantly,

your efforts will be in vane and make you look like a hypocrite.

If old feelings come back, repeat this process until you feel a since of freedom and openness toward that person.

Here are Some Questions to Ask Yourself to Start Forgiving Yourself and Others:

1. What are the names of the people you need to forgive?

   _____

   _____

2. What past offenses/people do you need to release before you can move forward in life?

   _____

   _____

3. What past negative situations do you hold yourself responsible for?

   _____

   _____

4. What are the names of the people you still hold

responsible for your past pain that you need to forgive?

_____

_____

5. What are 5 things you have learned from past offenses against you?

_____

_____

6. What are 5 things you have learned from your past offenses against others?

_____

_____

7. How has not letting go of past offenses affected your relationships?

_____

_____

The Seed of Action

1. Write down a list of 10 people you feel you need to forgive.

2. Write down a list of 10 people you want forgiveness from.

3. Write down 5 instances where not forgiving a person has hurt you in life (i.e., in a relationship, with your finances, in your career, discovering long-term happiness).

4. Follow the six steps to forgiveness.

5. Ask for forgiveness from the people you have offended.

6. Take a class/workshop on forgiveness.

7. Read a book that focuses on forgiveness, especially if you find it difficult to forgive anyone.

8. Commit to practicing forgiveness daily.

The Seed of Motivation and Inspiration

"It does not take courage to dream, but it does take courage to make a dream come true."

<u>The Difference Between Motivation and Inspiration</u>

Most people get up and go to work because they have to pay their bills, not because they love their job. The number one reason people continue to work at an unfavorable job is to avoid getting fired. In other words, the individual is *motivated* by the paycheck he receives and by the fear of being terminated from the job he detests. **Motivation** is the external driving force behind your decision to act on a situation—even situations that are unpleasant. But what if you loved your job so much that you could not wait to get to work every morning? You loved it so much that you laid out your clothing the night before, arrived at work one hour early to get started, and stayed late to discuss new ideas with senior staff about making the company more efficient. Notice there is no mention of compensation or fear. When you love your job and have a passionate approach to getting it done you begin to feel as if you were born to fulfill that role. In other words, you are *inspired* to fulfill the responsibilities of your position. **Inspiration** is the internal drive that compels you to go above and beyond the expectations of others.

Motivation is when you reach on the outside of yourself and *Inspiration* is when you reach on the inside of yourself.

Motivation is used to get things done in your life that you must do, such as paying bills so your credit score will remain favorable, losing weight to avoid hospitalization, buying your girlfriend an engagement ring so she does not leave, cooking your husband dinner so he doesn't eat out with someone else, or getting a new job because you can't afford to pay your bills with the job you have now. Motivation should only be used to make short-term changes, not long-term alterations to your lifestyle. Since motivation derives from the outside, it does not have permanency and it will not last long enough to sustain major life style changes. I often refer to it as *motivation through desperation.*

Where Does Motivation Come From?

Motivation derives from an external passion for attaining something you really want. It is the fuel needed to go after something you cannot picture your life without. When you are motivated you are energized and ready to spring into action. It is the desire to make something happen right now no matter what.

Motivation is the force behind your most accretive actions, constantly pushing you forward to achieve your goals and dreams. The force is uncontrollable and undeniable; it is destiny. Motivation is the fuel of achievers, historic conquerors, and everyone that desires to be great. The fuel is the matrix behind purposeful action and success. Motivation: you either have it or you don't.

Where Does Inspiration Come From?

Inspiration is similar to motivation except it comes from inside the person; it can last a lifetime and can be passed down from one generation to the next. Inspiration is the intrinsic reason behind what we do. It is the burning light in the dark when all hope is lost. Inspiration is a subtle nudge, that once applied can be the strong force it takes to try once more after endless defeats. It is hope even when your back is up against the ropes and it is the lifeline to our dreams. Inspiration is a strong internal push that makes sacrifice necessary, pain bearable, and life worth living. Inspiration: either you have it or you don't.

How to Find Motivation

Motivation is the bond found through spending quality time with something or someone you desire to have. It comes from taking the time to think about the outcome of a situation. Motivation is sparked when you recognize what you want and what you must have. You can find motivation by asking, "What's in it for me?" Ultimately motivation comes from a basic desire to have something in your possession within a relatively short time frame.

How to Find Inspiration

Inspiration is found in stories, artwork, nature or in poetry. It is found by recognizing the beauty of nature and it connects with something on the inside of you. It is an uncontrollable urge to take definite action. Inspiration is the GOD within us awakened. To find inspiration is to connect with the GOD within you.

When you have been touched by inspiration your life will never be the same. You will forever be quickened. In order to be inspired is to be awakened and to be willing to do whatever it takes no matter the price.

When a person is acting out of inspiration they are adhering to a higher authority. An inspired individual views their actions as necessary to accomplish a greater task for mankind instead of only being concerned with their own survival.

If you find motivation you can change your life. If you find inspiration you can change the world.

Motivation is when you work hard to make a million dollars for yourself, while inspiration is when you work hard to make a million dollars for a cause greater than you.

Motivation preserves your existence and enhances your own life, while inspiration creates a greater opportunity for others.

Here are Some Questions to Ask Yourself to Help You Find Motivation:

1. What gives you short term energy?

_____

_____

2. What would get you out of bed at 2am in the morning to work on?

_____

_____

3. What songs make you feel like you can do anything?

_____

_____

4. What is the thing that if someone said they would give it to you right now it would cause you to take immediate action?

_____

_____

<u>Here are Some Questions to Ask Yourself to Help You Find</u>
<u>Inspiration</u>:

1. What would you love to do more than anything else?

   _____

   _____

2. What would get you out of bed at 5am every morning to work on it?

   _____

   _____

3. What types of magazines steal your attention and cause you to daydream?

   _____

   _____

4. What draws so much of your attention that you lose track of time when you are engaged in doing it?

   _____

   _____

5. Who are the people that when you hear their story you

feel like you must take action.

_____

_____

6. What is the last book you read that made you feel good on the inside?

_____

_____

7. What songs make you feel like you have a purpose in life?

_____

_____

8. What recurring dreams and thoughts about doing something great do you have?

_____

_____

9. What are your God-given or innate talents and gifts?

_____

_____

10. How much time do you spend telling your story to help someone else and doing volunteer work?

_____

_____

11. What are you willing to sacrifice for now so you can have it later?

_____

_____

12. What are your greatest accomplishments?

_____

_____

13. If you only had 6 months to live what major cause would you give your life to?

_____

_____

Seeds of Action

1. Use the things that motivate you to take action daily.
2. Use the things that inspire you to change your life.

3. Spend time with people that motivate and inspire you.

4. Spend time engaging in activities that motivate and inspire you (i.e., listening to music, reading books, watching movies).

5. Find a purpose in life that is bigger than you. Find a purpose that will inspire others to follow or find someone else with a purpose that you can help them manifest.

6. Take a temperament assessment to help you find your God-given or innate talents, abilities, and gifts. You can find several on-line temperament assessment tools that you can use. The one I find most helpful is the Keirsey Temperament Sorter-II which can be found at www.advisorteam.com.

7. Volunteer your time to mentor a child or give money to a charitable cause you believe in.

8. Remember your greatest accomplishments and know that they are just the tip of the iceberg of what is possible for you.

The Seed of a Decision

"A decision is a silent commitment"

What is a Decision?

The word decision comes from a Latin word, *decisio*, which means to cut off and depart from. A decision is the ability to unwaveringly commit to an action that may be harmful or favorable to you and/or others. It is the ability to make "a cut," to get off of the fence, or to set a new course. In other words, make a conscious choice to get on with life. Making a decision is holding a proclamation without the need or desire for any additional information.

The Power of a Decision

Decisions are powerful beyond measure. When you make a decision you open the door to many opportunities. Most major movements throughout history were due to a decision. Decisions can win ballgames, make dreams come true, or destroy the bridge to a future of greatness.

If Frederick Douglass did not decide that slavery needed to be abolished, despite being a former slave, who knows when slavery would have ended? If Martin Luther King, Jr would have never decided to fight the injustice of racial prejudice, despite being 26 years old and facing physical danger, who knows how far the civil rights movement would have gone? If President Barack Obama did not decide to run for president of the United States, despite being relatively new to politics, who knows whom the United States' 44th president would have been? And, if I did not make a decision to write this book, in spite of being diagnosed with a learning disability, who knows what you would be reading right now?

"Facts do not discourage powerful decisions they only make them more powerful."

Lower vs. Higher Level Decisions

Higher level decisions are proactive, premeditated, and methodically planned decisions. These are the decisions that will secure your future for days, months, and even years to come. Higher-level decisions include going to college at an early age, purchasing a warranty or an insurance policy, purchasing a costly upgradeable electronic device, or choosing the proper spouse. Making higher-level decisions increase your chances of success and decrease your level of stress and drama. If you want to be successful, start making decisions that will secure your future. In order to make these decisions you must give up what you could have today for what you really want tomorrow. The person that strives for greatness makes a conscious effort to avoid making lower level decisions.

Lower level decisions are reactive decisions. Little thought or planning goes into making these types of decisions and they are usually made out of haste, pressure, and fear. Lower level decisions include purchasing a used tire when you really should plan for a new one; paying late fees for a bill; arguing with a person that you should not even have a relationship with; running out of gas because you didn't have time to stop at a gas station; and working a job that you dislike for five years. This is what I call the **rubber band effect**; this occurs when you stretch yourself to make a haste decision and the results snap back only to slap you in the face.

When I was three years old, my mother made the decision to settle my sister and I in an established middle class suburban neighborhood. Her decision not only set the course for how my sister and I would turn out, but also created a stable environment for growth, stability, and increased my possibilities for the future. Since she knew the importance of this decision, she eliminated all of the options for failure. For approximately 20 years she was steadfast to her decision. Her decision to move her family to the suburbs was at a higher level of consciousness; she made her decision based on the best place to raise her kids versus affordability. As a result, she did not have to make lower level decisions such as, "Is it safe enough to send my kids to the playground?", "Is the house next door a crack house?", or, "Will I have to purchase a gun to protect my family?" Due to her ability to make a higher-level decision, I have had the opportunity to experience a stable and healthy childhood that allowed me to find peace of mind although I struggled academically in school. Her decision served as a protective factor that buffered me from the hardship of growing up with a learning disability.

One higher-level decision can cancel out the need to make fifty lower level decisions. For example, let's say you decide to purchase a car that cost $300 a month but you decide not to purchase the extended warranty that covers all maintenance including breaks, windshield wipers, oil changes, and any other wear and tear items for an additional $55 per month. After 18 to 24 months you have to make lower level decisions on where to find the least expensive parts and least expensive mechanic to replace parts for your car. If you had made a decision to pay for the maintenance plan, you would not have to make anymore decisions on the maintenance of your car. When you make a proactive higher-level decision, you do not have to contemplate making lower level decisions that would not leverage your time, energy, or money but instead steal your time, energy, and money. I call this the process of *expansion*; to expand your future possibilities you must first make a decision to do so.

The Greatest Decision You Will Ever Make in Life
is Deciding Who You Are

It has been said by international motivational speaker, Les Brown that "God creates us but we make ourselves." I believe this statement is true because I also believe we are all made to be great. We have all the tools to get there, but unfortunately it takes time to develop and requires a conscious effort to apply the principles listed in this book. Making a decision about who you will become is consciousness in action. Have you ever thought about a person living in an unfavorable situation (i.e., drug addiction, unemployment, financial hardship, illness)? How many people do you believe consciously decided to endure those unfavorable situations? That is precisely the problem; they are not making conscious decisions about how they want to live their lives. Most of what they do everyday are based on lower-level decision-making. Unfortunately this is the norm for some people.

Deciding who you will become takes confidence, tenacity, a bit of faith, and most of all, it takes audacity. When a person decides who they will become, they wage war on the image of themselves that other people know and are comfortable with; that is because people resist the change that they see in your growth. It is similar to a caterpillar deciding that it wants to be a butterfly. The caterpillar that wants to become a butterfly should talk to other butterflies, not other caterpillars. The decision to chart your own course in life can be the most fearful journey you will ever embark on, but it will have been the most fulfilling.

The Cost of Making a Decision

When you decide to make a decision you risk the comfort of being liked, but you also escape mediocrity. When you defer or avoid making important decisions in your life it can cost you money, happiness, peace of mind, healthy relationships, your ability to be great and, possibly, life itself. When you avoid making important and powerful decisions, you can impede or derail your success. It may also keep you from walking in your greatness. Not only do you lose when you don't make an important and powerful decision, but the people looking up to you miss out on a testimony in action. *Remember, your decisions are bigger than you and they speak to everyone in your life!*

Reversing the Effects of an Unfavorable Decision

In order to reverse the effect of an unfavorable decision, you must desire change on a deep level and be willing to pay a greater price. Reversing the effects of an unfavorable decision can be difficult. It takes a clear vision of where you want to go and what you want to do, some blood, sweat and tears, and a lot of patience. Most of all, you will need to make sure you have enough time set aside in your life to make the change. You did not get into your situation overnight and you will not get out of your situation overnight. You will also need courage and a great support system to make sure you are successful at the change you are trying to bring about. The one thing you need more than anything else is God's favor and grace. Without that you will be working against yourself. Here are five steps to follow in order to reverse the effects of an unfavorable decision:

1. Come up with at least four different reasons why you want to make this change. Do not move forward until you are sure that this is what you want to do. Taking action without a strong motive can lead to frustration, wavering, disbelief from others, and ultimately failure.

2. Meditate and pray daily for divine guidance, clarity, truth, patience, and the will to be steadfast.

3. Become a student of the change you want to take place. Learn everything about what you want to happen. If you do this, you will start to breathe and live your change. When people see you they will think the change has already happened. At that point the change has no other choice but to take place, because you have induced it into your life.

4. Set aside some time out of each day to dedicate to your change. Most people will never change because they are not willing to make the time for the process of change. A caterpillar does not change into a butterfly overnight and neither will you.

5. Develop a support system just for the purpose of achieving this change. Your support system should include people that believe in you and what you are trying to accomplish. Your support should also include people that possess specialized knowledge about the change you are trying to create in your life. People love to talk about their achievements, so all you have to do is ask the right questions and listen.

The Fence

The fence is a place a lot of people find themselves when it comes to making important life-defining decisions. The fence is an uncomfortable, but very familiar place to anyone who is unable or unwilling to make a commitment. Many people say they want to change, but only the ones that are committed actually do.

The inability to make a serious decision in your life cannot only create stagnation but it can also prevent you from living your dreams and becoming happy and free of bondage. The inability to make decisions can also lead to serious problems in the areas of finances, relationships, physical health, mental health, education, and personal success. The inability to make a decision can waste valuable resources such as money, time and even healthy relationships. If you have a hard time making decisions then you probably have a hard time getting rid of clutter in your life. Physical clutter is symbolic of mental clutter.

The Seed of a Decision

A person that has a lot of unresolved mental baggage cannot move forward because most of their brain energy is spent on carrying mental baggage. Getting off the fence is more than just making choices. It is more about uncovering and releasing mental baggage that, for most people, stem from their childhood or early adult life. To start the process of uncovering and releasing mental baggage and to get off of the fence try the following steps:

1. Talk to an objective friend or relative that can give you sound advice about making difficult decisions and releasing past baggage.
2. Hire a Life Coach to help you make some critical life-changing decisions
3. Seek a Licensed Clinical Professional Counselor (LCPC) to work through deep-rooted childhood issues.
4. Read a couple of books, and or attend a workshop, on uncovering and releasing mental baggage.
5. Set deadlines on when you will make a decision on a couple of important issues you have been putting off for a while.
6. For each major issue you are facing, write down what you stand to lose and gain for each option you are considering then write down what you may lose if you make no decision.

Either you can make a conscious decision to get off the fence or life can make it for you. Even if you are a world-class gymnast you will not be able to stay on the fence forever. Either you can take control of your life and decide which side of the fence you want to land on, or you can opt to let the luck of the draw determine your destiny.

Here are Some Questions That Will Help You
Make Great Decisions:

1. Do you have difficulty making important decisions?

   _____

   _____

2. Do you defer making decisions because of fear on a daily basis?

   _____

   _____

3. What are some recent decisions that you have been putting off?

   _____

   _____

4. What favorable decisions have you made in the last 12 months?

   _____

   _____

5. What unfavorable decisions have you made in the last 12 months?

_____

_____

6. Do you like who you have become because of the decisions you have made in the past?

_____

_____

7. Who do you counsel with to help you make decisions?

_____

_____

8. How have your decisions shaped your life?

_____

_____

9. Other than you, who has benefited from your decisions?

_____

_____

10. Other than you, who has suffered from your decisions?

_____

_____

11. What do you need to cut out of your life and who do you need to spend less time communicating with?

_____

_____

12. How do you think the decisions that you are making today will shape your tomorrow?

_____

_____

The Seed of Action

1. Find a mentor or hire a life coach to help you start making decisions.
2. Keep a journal on the decisions you make and record the outcomes favorable or unfavorable.
3. List on a sheet of paper the things that you would like to become, then ask yourself what decisions must I make to become this?
4. Listen to self-help audio programs, inspirational music, and people that will motivate you to make the great decisions you need and want to make.

135

5. Find or read about people who have made similar decisions to the ones you want to make.

6. Clean a room in your house that is cluttered before you make a hard decision. This will clear your mind, free up mental energy and allow new ideas to flow.

<u>Recommended Resources</u>

Great Books

Bible

The Success Principles, How to Get from Where You
Are to Where You Want to Be
By Jack Canfield

Trash Man to the Cash Man
By Myron Golden

Who Moved My Cheese?
By Spencer Johnson, M.D.

Seven Spiritual Laws of Success
By Deepak Chopra

As a Man Thinketh
By James Allen

The Art of Happiness
By His Holiness, the Dalai Lama
and Howard C. Cutler. M.D.

A Setback Is a Setup for a Comeback
By Willie Jolley

The Book of Questions
By Gregory Stock, PH.D.

The Book of Positive Quotations
By John Cook

The Greatest Salesman in the World
By OG Mandino

THINK AND GROW RICH
By Napoleon Hill

It's Not Over Until You Win!
By Les Brown

The Twelve Universal Laws of Success
By Herbert Harris

The Seven Habits of Highly Effective People
By Stephen R. Covey

The Top 10 Distinctions Between Millionaires
and the Middle Class
By Keith Cameron Smith

The 21 Irrefutable Laws of Leadership
By John C. Maxwell

The Dip
A Little Book That Teaches You When to Quit
By Seth Godin

The Parent Connection, 20 Principles for Strong Parenting
By CJ Gross

Conversations with GOD
By Neale Donald Walsch

You Can Heal Your Life
By Louise Hay

Great Motivational, Inspiration and Informational CD's Programs

The Success Principles, How to Get from Where You
Are to Where You Want to Be
By Jack Canfield

It's Not Over Until You Win!
By Les Brown

Seven Spiritual Laws of Success
By Deepak Chopra

The Power of Purpose
By Les Brown

Awaken the Giant Within
By Anthony Robbins

The Seven Habits of Highly Effective People
By Stephen R. Covey

The Seasons of Life
By Jim Rohn

It Only Takes a Minute to Change Your Life

By Willie Jolley

The Parent Connection, 20 Principles for Strong Parenting

By CJ Gross

Conversations with GOD

By Neale Donald Walsch

You Can Heal Your Life

By Louise Hay

Great Inspirational and Life Enhancing Movies

Secretariat

Ray

Eat Pray Love

The Blind Side

Yes Man

The Karate kid

Erin Brockovich

Joe vs. the Volcano

The Ultimate Gift

Flash of Geniuses

Cast Away

The Pursuit of Happyness

The Shawshank Redemption

The Kite Runner

The Secret

School of Rock

Remember the Titans

Glory

The Hurricane

The Great Debaters

Seven Years in Tibet

Conversations with GOD

The Book of Eli

Gifted Hands

Great Personal Development Web Sites to Visit

Seeds of Life LLC

www.seedsoflifellc.com

Learning Annex

www.learningannex.com

Toast Masters International

www.toastmasters.org

The National Association of Women Business Owners

www.nawbo.org

Fabjobs

www.fabjobs.com

Entrepreneur

www.entrepreneur.com

Online Organizing

www.onlineorganizing.com

Success Television

www.successtelevision.com

Mind Tools

www.mindtools.com

Compass

www.mylifecompass.com

Volunteer Web Sites

US Dream Academy

www.usdreamacademy.org

Big Brothers Big Sisters

www.bbbs.org

Volunteer Match

www.volunteermatch.org

Habitat for Humanity

www.habitat.org

The National CARES Mentoring Movement

www.caresmentoring.com

Ameri Corps

www.americorps.gov

American Red Cross

www.redcross.org

Kiva

www.kiva.com

Find Your Mission

www.findyourmission.org

CPSIA information can be obtained
at www.ICGtesting.com
Printed in the USA
FFOW02n2206030315
11481FF

Kiva

www.kiva.com

Find Your Mission

www.findyourmission.org

Thank You

Thank you for taking the time to purchase and read this book. As you start to plant the life-guiding seeds from this book, you may encounter challenges and fears. Do not turn back or away from those challenges and fears, they are part of the process of making you great. From this day forward, walk in your greatness and know that a great life is possible!!!

If this book has helped you realize your dreams, achieve your goals, or gain more focus about what you want out of life, please send your testimony to seedsoflifellc@aol.com. We would love to hear from you. To book CJ Gross or order books please call 240-350-2147 or visit www.seedsoflifellc.com.

Blessings,

CJ Gross

Life Coach/Speaker/Author

CPSIA information can be obtained
at www.ICGtesting.com
Printed in the USA
FFOW02n2206030315
11481FF